LINKING LITERATURE WITH SELF-ESTEEM

Integrating Literature Into Basic Skills Programs

by Shirley Cook

Incentive Publications, Inc.
Nashville, Tennessee

Illustrated by Marta Johnson
Cover by Tony Novak
Edited by Jan Keeling

ISBN 0-86530-196-4

Table Of Contents

NOTES
FOR THE TEACHER

This book was written to help guide teachers in the selection of literature that can be integrated into any Language Arts Program to help build skills while directly dealing with issues of self-esteem.

In an attempt to integrate all areas of the curriculum rather than isolating one from another, LINKING LITERATURE WITH SELF-ESTEEM provides the teacher with a variety of possibilities for each literary selection. Vocabulary words can be discussed before reading or as the story is read. Students are given the opportunity to respond to each book with journal entries, integrating each story with personal experience. The journal entries are perfect springboards for esteem-building discussion.

Three additional activities are offered for linking each piece of literature to curriculum areas such as science, art, social studies, writing, and math. To make connections clear, a heading is included for each activity to show to which area it belongs. These activities accommodate a wide variety of learning styles as well as teaching styles, and may also be used for horizontal or vertical enrichment.

The Esteem Enhancer provides an activity that directly addresses issues of personal worth, family circumstances, hurt, and healing. Dealing with these issues is essential for building and maintaining healthy peer relationships as well as for enhancing individual self-esteem. With increasing numbers of young people struggling with concerns regarding self-worth, this guide will help every educator open the door to our most important job as teachers—helping each and every child feel valued and loved.

INDIVIDUAL DIFFERENCES

Anna Banana And Me

by Lenore Blegvad

Name _____

SUMMARY

Anna Banana's bravery and carefree spirit hold her shy young friend in awe.

VOCABULARY

1. fountain
2. statue
3. scuffles
4. staircase

5. galloping
6. bannister
7. pretend
8. moat

9. turret
10. goblin
11. enormous
12. horrible

JOURNAL ENTRY

Choose one of the following topics to write about:
1. The bravest thing I have ever done.
2. My friend and I are quite different.
3. My most frightening memory.

_____

_____

_____

_____

_____

_____

CURRICULUM INTEGRATION

THINKING SKILLS
Anna Banana is a rhyming, sing-song sort of name. Take the first name of each of your classmates and make up a rhyming name phrase that is creative and positive. Example: Bill has a lot of skill.

THINKING SKILLS
Anna Banana says, "A feather is magic!" Write a story entitled "The Magic Feather." Use yourself as one of the main characters.

WRITING
Pretend that you have a magic feather that gives you the power to fly. Your journey will take twelve hours. As you float through space, draw a map of the places over which you fly. Label each place on the map.

ESTEEM ENHANCER

Using the puppet pattern provided, create a brave and confident new puppet. Give your puppet a name. Then get together with a friend and put together a skit about two friends who are very different from each other.

Puppet Pattern

Different, Not Dumb

by Margot Marek

Name _____

SUMMARY

Jeff and Mike are two friends with big differences in their reading abilities. When a dangerous situation arises, however, the boys pool their reading skills to prevent a tragedy from occurring.

VOCABULARY

1. forehead
2. balanced
3. alphabet
4. pretended

JOURNAL ENTRY

We all have subjects at school in which we do very well and subjects in which we don't do as well. Write about the subjects in which you do well, and tell why you feel you do well in them.

_____

_____

_____

_____

_____

_____

_____

CURRICULUM INTEGRATION

WRITING

The illustrations for this story are photographs rather than drawings. Bring one of your favorite photographs to class and write a short story about it.

POETRY

Mike learned to memorize letters and their sounds in order to become a better reader. Choose a poem and memorize it as an exercise in memory improvement. The poem should have eight or more lines.

SCIENCE

Do some research to find out what causes an explosion. Conduct the following simple experiment to create a non-threatening, somewhat explosive chemical reaction. You will need:

> 1 bottle with a cork
> ½ cup vinegar
> ½ cup water
> 2 tablespoons baking soda
> paper toweling

Place the baking soda in a piece of paper toweling and twist the towel around the soda into a long pencil-like shape. Mix the vinegar and water and place it in the bottle. Add the soda-pencil and quickly place the cork on top. Watch to see what happens to the cork.

ESTEEM ENHANCER

Design a patchwork quilt with the most difficult words that you know how to read. Color it as brightly as you would want your quilt to be.

Nobody's Perfect, Not Even My Mother

by Norma Simon

Name _____

SUMMARY

A beautiful account of how all people are good at some things, but everyone is different. None of us is perfect, and that's perfectly okay.

VOCABULARY

1. perfect
2. exactly
3. somersaults
4. machines
5. especially
6. dinosaur
7. Vietnamese

JOURNAL ENTRY

Everyone has different strengths and weaknesses. Write about the different strengths each member of your family has.

_____

_____

_____

_____

_____

_____

_____

CURRICULUM INTEGRATION

THINKING SKILLS
List as many skills as you can think of that you have acquired so far in your life.

THINKING SKILLS
The members of your family all have certain skills and abilities. If you could add new members to your family tree while keeping all of your present family, who would your top five choices be? You can add anyone you like—friends, famous personalities, athletes, singers, or neighbors. Use the worksheet titled "Family Tree." Write something about each addition to explain your choice. For example, if you add Whitney Houston to your family tree, you may write "beautiful singer" under her name.

WRITING
Some families feel a need to behave more perfectly than others because the public is constantly watching them. Write a story about how your life would be changed if you were a member of Great Britain's Royal Family.

ESTEEM ENHANCER

Interview another member of your class. Prepare ten questions to ask in your interview such as, "What hobbies do you enjoy?" Write down the answers to each of the questions as your partner answers them. Next, write a story about the differences between you and your interview partner. How would you like to be more like him or her?

Family Tree

List the members of your family on the tree trunk, then add five "new family members" to their spots.

Write something about each to explain your choice.

My Present Family

1. - - - - - - - - - -

2. - - - - - - - - - -

3. - - - - - - - - - -

4. - - - - - - - - - -

5. - - - - - - - - - -

Arnie And The New Kid

by Nancy Carlson

Name _____

SUMMARY

After suffering an unfortunate accident, Arnie learns to empathize with Philip, who is bound to a wheelchair.

VOCABULARY

1. wheelchair
2. hospital
3. sprained
4. complained
5. challenged
6. collection
7. computer
8. condition

JOURNAL ENTRY

Philip is not able to do the same things that Arnie does because he must remain in his wheelchair. Explain in as much detail as possible all of the changes you would experience if you had to rely on a wheelchair instead of your legs.

_____

_____

_____

_____

_____

_____

_____

_____

CURRICULUM INTEGRATION

SCIENCE
Design the super wheelchair of the future. What novel features would it have? Draw it and label its important features.

PHYSICAL EDUCATION
Invent a new sport that kids in wheelchairs could play with able-bodied kids. Write out detailed rules. Be sure to give the sport a name.

MATH
Borrow a wheelchair from the nurse's office. Have each member of the class take turns wheeling a specific number of yards in the hallway. Time each person, and record the times. Figure the average time it takes for each student to travel the distance. Create five other math problems with the data you have gathered.

ESTEEM ENHANCER

Try your hand at Cooperative Circles. The class may work together in one circle or be divided up into two or three circles. Important rules for each cooperative circle are:

1. Never use put downs.
2. Take turns.
3. Stay in your place.
4. Be a good listener.
5. Plan your comments (pass if you must).

Members of a cooperative circle are given an activity to complete or a question to discuss. Younger children may need a cue to help them realize when it is their turn. For example, they may pass an object from person to person as each one contributes (decide on an object to pass from person to person before the activity begins). Suggested question for a Cooperative Circle: **What type of handicap would be the most difficult to live with and why?** Younger children may wish to draw pictures of their responses before getting into their Cooperative Circle. A representative of each group should tell the class the results of the circle discussion.

Everyone Is Special

by Marcia Neese

Name _____

SUMMARY

Timmy and his father both learn that everyone is special in some way, and people should never be judged on the basis of their color.

VOCABULARY

1. exclaimed
2. beautiful
3. canopy
4. supposed
5. suggested
6. decided
7. peddled
8. whispered
9. introduce
10. relieved
11. cafeteria
12. individual
13. styrofoam
14. announcement
15. disappointed
16. deserved
17. conversation
18. boulder

JOURNAL ENTRY

All of us know people who are not very well-liked. Why do you think some people seem to be more popular than others? Why is it important to so many people to be well-liked?

_____

_____

_____

_____

_____

_____

CURRICULUM INTEGRATION

SOCIAL STUDIES
A stereotype is an idea that people have that makes the members of one group of people or of one group of things all exactly alike. An example is the *Blonde Stereotype* that says that all blondes are dumb. In the story "Everyone Is Special," black people are also stereotyped as dumb. What other stereotypes can you think of? Name at least two. Then give an example that shows that each stereotype is not true.

SCIENCE
It is interesting to know that some types of paint "melt" styrofoam. Conduct the following experiment on the reactions of paints to various materials. You will need plastic, tinfoil, a small piece of wood, a ceramic plate, watercolor paint, tempera paint, latex paint, and oil-based paint. Apply a small amount of each paint to a different area of each of the four materials. Then fill out a chart showing which paint works best on each surface (use the illustration as a model). Some paints may work well on several types of surfaces.

SURFACES	PAINTS			
	oil	watercolor	tempera	latex
Plastic				
Wood				
Tin-foil				
Ceramic				

ART/WRITING
Draw a new member of the Boulder Gang who looks similar to the other characters drawn by Neese. Tell how this new friend would be special.

COOPERATION

A Weekend With Wendell

by Kevin Henkes

Name _____

SUMMARY

When Wendell comes to stay with Sophie while his parents visit out-of-town relatives, he proves to be a rather uncooperative guest.

VOCABULARY

1. relatives
2. pretended
3. allergic
4. whispered

JOURNAL ENTRY

Wendell was having a wonderful weekend at Sophie's until Sophie began making the rules. Tell about your favorite weekend away from home. Where did you go, and what did you do?

_____

_____

_____

_____

_____

_____

_____

CURRICULUM INTEGRATION

THINKING SKILLS
You have been asked to babysit for Wendell for the evening. Describe four games that you would be prepared to play with Wendell. What things would you take with you in your babysitter's kit?

WRITING
You are a toy designer for a major toy company. Create an ad for your latest toy. Write a paragraph of information outlining its special features. Sketch your toy for the ad.

SCIENCE/ART
Clean out a small milk carton from your school lunch. Cut off the top. Put in 6 to 10 broken old crayons of various colors. Set the carton in the sun. (Make sure all paper has been removed from around the crayons.) When the crayons have melted, let them cool. Peel the milk carton from around your new multi-colored crayon. Use it to draw a picture of a game that you would play with Wendell.

ESTEEM ENHANCER

Create a Cooperation Candle. Write as many phrases and words on the candle as you can think of that show cooperation. During the week, as you use the words and phrases with someone else, or as another person uses them with you, cut them one at a time from your candle. If your candle burns down completely, you will have had a wonderfully cooperative week.

Crabby Gabby

by Stephen Cosgrove

Name _____

SUMMARY

Gabby, the Furry Eyeball, insists on having her own way and is selfish and intolerant of the opinions of others. Kartusch, the gentle, slithering, blind snake, helps her determine the error of her ways.

VOCABULARY

1. mystical
2. magical
3. suggestions
4. requests
5. demands
6. peacocks
7. meadow moss
8. fit to be tied
9. sarcastically
10. stately
11. idly
12. selfish
13. enjoyment
14. victory

JOURNAL ENTRY

Think about a time when you may have behaved selfishly or may have been crabby with someone. Tell about it. How do you think the people with you felt? What do you think you could do differently the next time something similar happens to you?

_____

_____

_____

_____

_____

_____

_____

CURRICULUM INTEGRATION

THINKING SKILLS
Gabby began by making suggestions to others, then advanced to making requests of others, then began making demands. Compare suggestions, requests, and demands. Tell how they are different. Tell about times when you have made each one.

ART/DRAMA
Create a Furry Eyeball using pom pons, felt, pipe cleaners, and wiggly eyes. After you have named your Furry Eyeball, make a list of the characteristics that he or she has. Then get together with a friend and create a dialogue between your two new creations.

ESTEEM ENHANCER

Work in a cooperative group to create solutions for the following problems. Make sure that all members contribute to and agree with each solution.

1. Your older brother John has just gotten a brand-new mountain bike. You and John always share your new toys with each other. However, last time you borrowed his remote-controlled airplane, you accidentally broke it. Now John has told you that he will never allow you to borrow his new bike. You have already promised your best friends that you will ride it to their houses and show it to them. What can you do and say to convince John that you should be allowed to borrow his bicycle?

2. Ruth Ann is the new girl in the class. She is bossy and always wants her own way. The big track meet for your school is about to take place and your class has been divided into four teams. Ruth Ann is on your team and immediately begins to boss everyone around. Even though she is not very good in the high jump or the hurdles, she has told everyone that she will handle those events. Only one person from each team may participate in each event. You and your friends would like Ruth Ann to be in different events, but she refuses. Your teacher has told you to solve the problem on your own. What will you do?

3. You have always been best friends with John and Billy. You all live on the same street and spend a lot of time together. Lately John has made a lot of suggestions about things for the three of you to do that you do not really like. Billy seems to want to do everything John suggests, and neither of them seems to be at all interested in your ideas anymore. You really want to be part of John and Billy's activities but would like to have some of your own suggestions followed, too. What can you do to get your friends to listen to you?

The Terrible Thing That Happened At Our House

by Marge Blaine

Name _____

SUMMARY

A family learns the importance of cooperation when Mom returns to her job as a science teacher.

VOCABULARY

1. important
2. frankfurters
3. annoying
4. salmon croquettes
5. serviced
6. decided

JOURNAL ENTRY

Everyone in the family in this story had to help by doing certain chores around the house. What chores do you do to help your family? What other chores could you do to help out? Which chores are your favorite ones?

_____

_____

_____

_____

_____

_____

_____

CURRICULUM INTEGRATION

HEALTH

Organization is important when a family cooperates to get the family chores done. It is also important to spend time at your job or school as well as to provide time for recreation and exercise. Create a chart for yourself that outlines how you will spend a typical day in order to get in all of the activities that you need. Be sure to allow 8 to 9 hours for sleep.

Example:

TIME	ACTIVITY
9:00 p.m. to 6:00 a.m.	Sleep
6:00 p.m. to 7:30 a.m.	Get ready for school, eat breakfast

THINKING SKILLS

Suggest five new titles for this book. Rank order them from your favorite to least favorite.

SCIENCE

With so many families having mothers and fathers with jobs outside the home, the modern time-saving conveniences (such as microwave ovens) are very important to them. Design a new time-saving invention that would be of value to a busy family. Draw a picture of your invention and write a paragraph describing its features.

ESTEEM ENHANCER

In a cooperative group of three or four, discuss the following problems and come up with solutions on which everyone can agree. Take turns writing down your group's ideas.

1. You are eleven years old, and your brother Ben is four. It is your job to babysit for Ben every day after school from 4:00 to 6:00 until your father gets home. On Friday your best friend is having a birthday party at the Pizza Arcade from 4:00 to 7:00. You really want to go, but you know that your family can't afford to hire a babysitter and is really depending on you. What should you do?

2. You are in a cooperative group that works on science projects together. There are three people in your group. You and your friend Michael work very hard to get your experiments done and your lab sheets turned in on time. Your other partner, Joanne, is a real time-waster. Whenever the teacher comes to check on your group, Joanne makes it sound as though she has done everything. Your group grades are excellent, but you and Michael are fed up. You know that the teacher really likes Joanne because she is the principal's daughter. What should you do?

Making The Team

by Nancy Carlson

Name _____

SUMMARY

Louanne and Arnie work together to try out for the cheerleading squad and the football team with surprising results.

VOCABULARY

1. exciting
2. cheerleading
3. practice
4. cartwheels

5. ought
6. tackling
7. improve
8. rarely

9. encouraged
10. confidence

JOURNAL ENTRY

When you get into high school, you will need to choose the sports and extra-curricular activities in which you would like to participate. Which activities do you think you will choose? Why?

_____

_____

_____

_____

_____

_____

_____

CURRICULUM INTEGRATION

PHYSICAL EDUCATION
Invent a new sport or extracurricular activity that you would like to see the high schools of the future offer to students. Describe it in detail by telling who could participate, skills required, how the sport would be played, or the purpose of the activity. Be creative. The sky is the limit.

THINKING SKILLS
Louanne and Arnie make a great twosome. List as many other things as you can think of that are found in twos.

WRITING
Write a paragraph of information telling how you feel about the following statement: All girls and boys should be allowed to play in all sports and join in all clubs and activities that they personally choose.

ESTEEM ENHANCER

Write the word COOPERATION vertically. Then create a cooperation word poem of phrases or words that describe cooperative attitudes and activities by using the letters as shown in the example.

C
O
O
P
Everyone working together willingly
R
A
Telling a friend that his or her work is good
I
O
N

Gus And Buster Work Things Out

by Andrew Bronin

Name _____

SUMMARY

Chapter 4, "The Television Set": Gus and Buster each wish to watch a different television program at the same time. During their argument, the knob is broken off the television. Gus and Buster eventually cooperate and work things out.

VOCABULARY

1. refrigerator
2. soda
3. helmet
4. pretzels
5. purpose

JOURNAL ENTRY

Describe a disagreement that you had with a member of your family and tell how you were able to work it out.

_____

_____

_____

_____

_____

_____

_____

CURRICULUM INTEGRATION

SOCIAL STUDIES

Survey your class to find out everyone's favorite spectator sports and everyone's favorite participant sports. Graph your results by coloring in the proper numbers of squares on charts similar to those illustrated below.

Favorite Spectator Sports

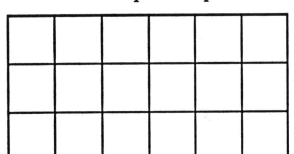

Favorite Participant Sports

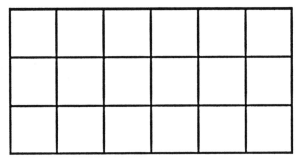

READING/DRAMA

Read another chapter of *Gus And Buster Work Things Out* with a friend. Prepare a dialogue and perform the chapter for a group or for your class.

WRITING

Write a new chapter for this book using one of the following chapter titles·

Gus Teaches Buster To Subtract
Gus and Buster At The Movies
Gus And Buster Go Swimming
Gus And Buster Meet A Friend

ESTEEM ENHANCER

Create a Positive Category Game Chart for your family. List the members of your family down the side. Be sure to include yourself. Then think of one positive word for each letter on the category chart to describe that person.

Example:

NAME	S	L	F	M
Bobby	smart	likeable	friendly	merry

SADNESS

A Fish In His Pocket

by Denys Cazet

Name _____

SUMMARY

When Russell's arithmetic book accidentally falls into the pond on his way to school, he has no idea of the sadness that awaits him.

VOCABULARY

1. November
2. grove
3. arithmetic
4. soggy

5. trudged
6. accident
7. attention
8. oozed

9. purpose
10. radiator

JOURNAL ENTRY

Russell needs to try to make things better for the little fish accidentally trapped in his arithmetic book. He builds his paper boat "Take Care" to send the fish back to its pond. Describe an accident that you were involved in and what you did (or what you could have done) to make the situation better.

_____

_____

_____

_____

_____

_____

_____

CURRICULUM INTEGRATION

THINKING SKILLS
A rebus is a story told with pictures and words. Tell part of Russell's story in rebus form. You may want to change or add to the story when you create your rebus.

Example:

WRITING
Write out the dialogue that might occur between Russell and a friend as he tells his friend of his day at school. What could his friend say to comfort him? Act out the dialogue with a friend.

MATH
Create some fishy math story problems. Each problem should involve both addition and subtraction.

ESTEEM ENHANCER

Create a poster of happy things that could be used to cheer up someone who is feeling sad. Arrange the following headings on the poster with appropriate illustrations under each heading:

This Is How I Look When I'm Happy...
Things That Make Me Feel Happy...
These Are Times When I Have Felt Happy...
People That Make Me Happy...

Alexander And The Terrible, Horrible, No Good, Very Bad Day

by Judith Viorst

Name _____

SUMMARY

It was simply a terrible, horrible, no good, very bad day from sunrise to sunset. Some days are like that—even in Australia.

VOCABULARY

1. Corvette
2. undercover
3. agent

4. Australia
5. scrunched
6. invisible

7. sprinkle
8. elevator
9. copying

JOURNAL ENTRY

Describe in detail the worst day that you can remember or the best day that you can remember.

_____

_____

_____

_____

_____

_____

CURRICULUM INTEGRATION

HEALTH
Alexander was unhappy when his mother forgot to pack his dessert. If you were in charge of making your own lunch for five days, and Mom and Dad would buy whatever you needed to make the lunches, what would you pack each day? Each lunch must contain five items and be well-balanced and healthful.

Example:

MONDAY	TUESDAY	WEDNESDAY	THURSDAY	FRIDAY
1. Milk
2. Tuna sandwich
3. Corn chips
4. Carrots
5. Cookies

VOCABULARY DEVELOPMENT
Make as many words as you possibly can from the letters in the name Alexander.

THINKING SKILLS
Think up titles for six new songs that deal with having a good day.

ESTEEM ENHANCER

Make up your own dictionary of new words that mean the following:

1. a terrible, no good, very bad day
2. a clumsy child
3. a lunch with no dessert
4. a breakfast cereal that doesn't taste good and doesn't have a prize
5. a lumpy pillow
6. a third-best friend
7. a mouth with a cavity
8. a fall in the mud
9. sneakers you don't like
10. green vegetables that you don't like

Then think of and write about a positive way to deal with each one so that it would not be a problem for you.

Sometimes I Like To Cry

by Elizabeth and Henry Stanton

Name _____

SUMMARY

A young boy explains how tears can be tears of fear, anger, sadness, and even tears of happiness.

VOCABULARY

1. toothy
2. scowl
3. sniffle

JOURNAL ENTRY

Oftentimes we think of sadness when we think of crying. Write about a time when you cried when you were not feeling sad. How do you feel when you are all finished crying?

_____

_____

_____

_____

_____

_____

_____

CURRICULUM INTEGRATION

SCIENCE
Do some research to find out how tears are produced by the eyes and what causes them to form. If possible, examine a tear under the microscope.

WRITING
The book *Sometimes I Like To Cry* was written to show that it's okay to cry. It also gives different reasons for crying. Create a new story entitled *Sometimes I Like To Laugh*. Think of all of the possible reasons for laughter. For example, do you ever laugh when you're nervous or afraid? Be sure to create a definite ending for your story. Illustrate it when you are finished.

THINKING SKILLS
Brainstorm with a friend to create a list of all the ways our lives would change if no one ever cried or laughed again. Share your list with another group or with the class.

Example:

IF NO ONE EVER CRIED OR LAUGHED AGAIN

1. Comedians would never know if their jokes were funny or not.
2.
3.

ESTEEM ENHANCER

Sadness can be overcome by thinking positively. Try your best to enjoy all that life has given you. In times of sadness it helps to have a cheerful phrase or motto to hold onto and repeat to yourself. Write a motto that you think will help to cheer you if you are feeling down. Make a cheerful, colorful banner of your phrase to hang someplace in your room at home.

Example: *Keep a poem in your pocket and a rainbow in your heart, and the blues will never start.*

Grandmama's Joy

by Eloise Greenfield

Name _____

SUMMARY

Grandmama feels sad that she and Rhondy must leave their home because the rent has become too much for her. Rhondy finally helps her to realize that as long as they have each other, everything will be fine.

VOCABULARY

1. plaid
2. audience
3. faraway
4. zinnias
5. crumpling
6. peppermint

JOURNAL ENTRY

Write about a favorite memory you have about something that you have done with one of your grandparents.

_____

_____

_____

_____

_____

_____

_____

_____

CURRICULUM INTEGRATION

SCIENCE

Rhondy's grandmama drank peppermint tea in the story. Experiment to find out how differently-flavored teas taste and which taste you prefer. You will need:

Instant tea	1 lemon	Peppermint extract
Water	1 lime	Strawberry extract
Sugar	1 orange	Almond extract

Mix tea according to the directions on the jar. Make one quart. Pour six glasses of tea. Into each glass add one of the flavors. (Squeeze the fresh fruit into the tea. Use an eye dropper to add one or two drops of each different extract.) Mix thoroughly after each addition. Sample each tea, and rank them in order of your preference.

DRAMA

Rhondy pretended to be a famous singer performing for her grandmother in order to try to cheer up her grandmama. Bring in a recording of a favorite song and practice a "lip sync" presentation to go along with the song. Try to imitate the motions of the performer singing the song. You may wish to include some simple costuming or prop ideas. After practicing and polishing up your act, you may wish to perform for the class.

SOCIAL STUDIES

Older American citizens may face financial problems like Rhondy's grandmama as prices continue to rise while their incomes do not. Make a list of all of the expenses that an average family has each month. Next to each item, make your best guess about just how much it would cost for one month.

Example: Family of 4 people
1. Groceries $400
2.
3.

ESTEEM ENHANCER

Rhondy looked in the yard for something to cheer up her grandmama. She finally brought in a sparkling stone. Create a list of "Cheerer Uppers" that you could try with family and friends. Then create a list of "Cheerer Uppers" that would help to cheer you up.

Example:

Cheerer Uppers For Family And Friends
1. Giving a big hug
2. Helping with chores without being asked
3.
4.

My Cheerer Uppers
1. Dad or Mom playing ball with me
2. Taking the puppy for a walk
3.
4.

The Tenth Good Thing About Barney

by Judith Viorst

Name _____

SUMMARY

When a young boy's cat, Barney, dies, the boy finds comfort in thinking about ten good things about his pet.

VOCABULARY

1. funeral
2. pussywillow
3. orangeade
4. absolutely

JOURNAL ENTRY

Think of ten good reasons that you could give your parents for allowing you to have a pet, if you had never had a pet of your own and very much wanted to have one. List them.

_____

_____

_____

_____

_____

_____

_____

_____

CURRICULUM INTEGRATION

WRITING/ART
Using magazine pictures, create a new kind of pet by gluing together parts of at least four different pictures. Write a story describing your pet and telling others why it would be a great pet to own.

READING
Make a list of twenty good books that have animals as characters. Be sure to list the authors as well. Then tell which book on the list, of the ones that you have read, is your favorite, and tell why it is your favorite.

WRITING
The mayor and city council have recently met and have informed the city that beginning next month only one kind of pet will be permitted within the city limits. They are asking the townspeople to vote on the kind of animal they feel should be allowed. The choices have been narrowed down to dogs, cats, and birds. You need to write an editorial for the town newspaper trying to convince others to support your choice.

ESTEEM ENHANCER

Fold a piece of paper in half vertically. At the top of the left half, write this title: **Things that don't make me feel better.** At the top of the right half, write this title: **Things that make me feel happy when I am sad.** Fill in this chart with as many ideas as possible.

ANGER

Sometimes It's O.K. To Be Angry

by Dr. Mitch Golant

Name _____

SUMMARY

Chapter five is a series of stories about children who become angry in a variety of situations. Suggestions for dealing with anger are made by characters, within the context of the story. The author then asks for input from the reader or the reader's audience. A wide variety of anger-producing situations are covered.

VOCABULARY

Selection will vary from
chapter to chapter.

JOURNAL ENTRY

Describe a time when you felt angry. How did you handle your anger? What could you have done differently?

_____

_____

_____

_____

_____

_____

_____

CURRICULUM INTEGRATION

THINKING SKILLS
Anger is an emotion that is felt by people. Think creatively to describe happenings that *don't* involve people, but that seem to express anger. List six to ten ideas. Illustrate your favorite.

Example: A bolt of lightning jumps from the sky and strikes a tree.

SCIENCE
Scientists have long studied the ways emotions can affect a person's health. Do some research to see what you can find out about anger and good health. Share your findings with your class.

WRITING
Rewrite Harriet's story from chapter 5 so that Harriet does not lose her temper with the dog.

ESTEEM ENHANCER

Create an "I Can Control My Anger" medal. After cutting out your medal, list three goals that you feel will help you remain in control when you feel yourself becoming angry. Keep your medal close by.

I'll Fix Anthony

by Judith Viorst

Name _____

SUMMARY

Anthony seems to be the big, mean brother.
Although his younger brother is too little to be
able to do much to control his big brother's behavior, he can think of lots of ways
he'll get even when he turns six.

VOCABULARY

1. clobber
2. sword
3. virus
4. German measles
5. wobble
6. fireplug
7. groceries
8. supermarket

JOURNAL ENTRY

It is often said that the oldest child is given, and can handle, more responsibility than
the younger ones. The youngest child is said to be spoiled. The middle child doesn't
seem to have to work as hard as the oldest and has more freedom than the youngest
child. Which position do you have in your family? How do you view your position,
and how does it compare to the positions of your brother(s) and sister(s)?

_____

_____

_____

_____

_____

_____

CURRICULUM INTEGRATION

WRITING

It is always fun to write a "Dear Judith Viorst" letter. Tell the author what you enjoyed most about the story, how it may relate to your life, if there were any parts of the story that you would change, as well as any questions that you would like to ask her. Mail the letter in care of her publisher.

THINKING SKILLS

The younger brother in the story felt that it was an important sign of being grown up when you could tell left from right. If you were in charge of teaching a group of ten young kids to learn left from right, what would you do? Design a game that you could play with them. Write down your instructions. Try the game on a younger child to see if it works.

HEALTH

Anthony's younger brother wanted to eat healthful foods that would make him strong. Put together a five-day health-food menu for him.

ESTEEM ENHANCER

Anthony's younger brother wanted to do certain things better than his brother, things like adding numbers in his mind. Make a list of ten things that you would like to be able to do better. Then, instead of just wishing they would happen, choose one idea from your list and make some goals that will allow you to achieve your wish.

Example:

WISH	GOALS
To be able to run faster	1. Run one mile every day for the next four weeks.
	2. Get plenty of rest.
	3. Eat properly.
	4. Time runs each day and record improvements.

The Black Snowman

by Phil Mendez

Name _____

SUMMARY

Jacob hates being black. He hates being black and poor. He hates everything black, until the magic of the kente restores his pride.

VOCABULARY

1. Africa
2. Anansi
3. Ashanti
4. kente
5. transforms
6. native
7. restores
8. ritual
9. invaders
10. seize
11. fray
12. vast
13. discarded
14. possesses
15. furious
16. lasso
17. interrupted
18. imagination
19. masterpiece
20. dissolved
21. exploded
22. retreated
23. generations
24. draped
25. suspiciously
26. impolite
27. concentration
28. forefathers
29. accepted
30. ordinary
31. confusing
32. warrior
33. approached
34. dislodged
35. scholars
36. Timbuktu
37. Bornu
38. descent
39. heritage
40. explosion
41. abandoned
42. devoured
43. collapsed
44. consumed
45. debris
46. evaporated

JOURNAL ENTRY

Jacob's heritage was very important to him. What do you know about your heritage?

_____

_____

_____

CURRICULUM INTEGRATION

WRITING
The magic kente came to America from Africa and was passed from person to person for hundreds of years. Tell the story of one family who had the kente before Jacob and Peewee.

THINKING SKILLS
Peewee very much wanted to buy a special Christmas gift for his mother, but he didn't have any money. What kinds of activities could elementary-school-age kids become involved in to earn money? Survey your class to gather as many ideas as possible. Chart your results.

MUSIC
Compose a song that tells about the story of "The Black Snowman."

ESTEEM ENHANCER

Create a personal coat of arms to reflect your heritage and your beliefs.

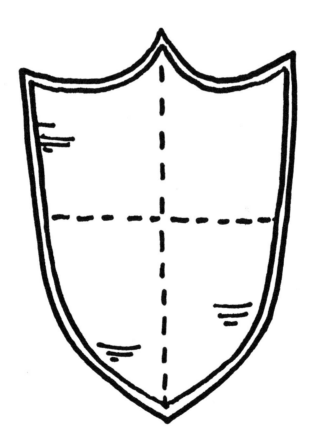

Attila The Angry

by Marjorie Weinman Sharmat

Name _____

SUMMARY

Attila is a frequently-angry squirrel whose anger causes his friends much distress. Then he attends a meeting of "Angry Animals Anonymous" and learns to squash, stamp out, and demolish angry thoughts—almost!

VOCABULARY

1. particularly
2. ranting, raving
3. furious
4. deserted
5. anonymous
6. squashed
7. demolished
8. ordinarily
9. appreciate
10. desperately
11. blasting
12. clutching
13. satisfied
14. pester
15. blazing

JOURNAL ENTRY

Some of the things that Attila got angry about were dust, trees, scissors, toothpicks, and chicken pox. What are some of the things that make you angry? What are some things you do to try to keep from becoming angry?

_____

_____

_____

_____

_____

_____

_____

CURRICULUM INTEGRATION

WRITING

One of the ways that Attila tried to control his anger was to prepare a meal of his favorite foods and invite his friends to join him. Make up an invitation to show how you would create your favorite meal to share with your friends. It may look something like this:

Dear_____,

Please join me for lunch!
I plan to serve:
1._____ 2._____
3._____

My other guests will be:
1._____
2._____
3._____
4._____

at_____ o'clock
R.S.V.P.

Sincerely,

THINKING SKILLS

Selling anything door to door, as Rusty and Marcy did with tickets, is a difficult job. Pretend that you are selling tickets for a band concert in your neighborhood. Write down what you would say or do that might help you with your sales.

WRITING

If anger was a disease instead of an emotion, and you were a well-known doctor, how would you cure your angry patients? Write out your cure, and share it with a friend.

ESTEEM ENHANCER

Each day for one week, check to see how angry you have gotten during the day. Use the ANGER THERMOMETER CHART to record your findings. Examine the reasons for your anger, and brainstorm with a group of friends in order to decide on ways you could have better handled your anger. Some ideas that have helped others are:
1. Draw an angry picture.
2. Sing a very loud but happy song.
3. Exercise briskly or run.

Anger Thermometer Chart

Use this chart to record how angry you get during one week, marking the "anger thermometer" for each day. 0 = No Anger and 10 = Extreme Anger. Examine the reasons for your anger and list them for each day. Brainstorm with a group of friends to come up with ways you could have better handled your anger; list them for each day.

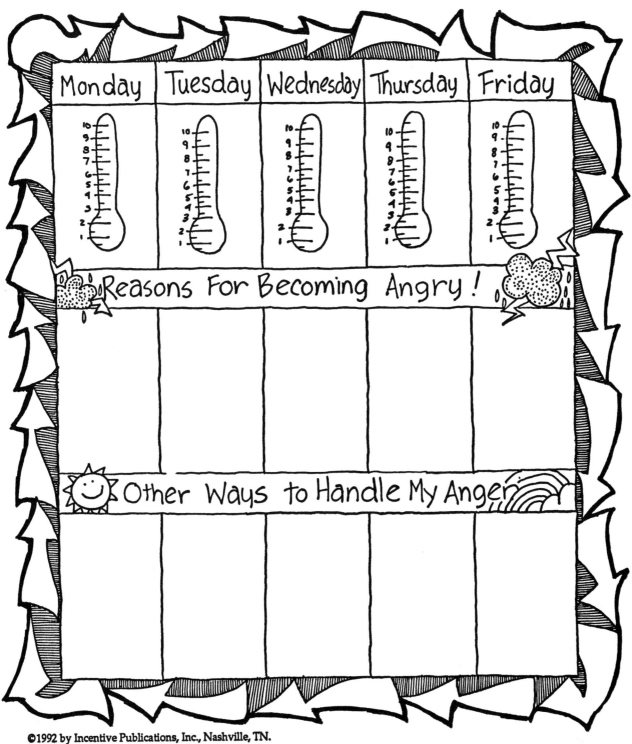

I Was So Mad

by Mercer Mayer

Name _____

SUMMARY

Little Critter's family just won't let him do anything that he wants to do. This makes him mad enough to run away—almost!

VOCABULARY

1. decided
2. decorate
3. practice

JOURNAL ENTRY

Most children probably think about running away from home at some time during their childhoods. A friend has just told you of plans to run away. Write a letter in which you try to convince him or her that this is not a good idea.

_____

_____

_____

_____

_____

_____

_____

CURRICULUM INTEGRATION

PHYSICAL EDUCATION
Little Critter wasn't a very successful juggler. Try your hand at juggling 2 balls or 3 balls. Your library may have a book on juggling to help you. You may also wish to talk with your gym teacher to gain some pointers.

VOCABULARY DEVELOPMENT
Brainstorm with a friend to create a list of words that would describe a person who is angry. (Examples: upset, miserable, out-of-control.) Try to find magazine or newspaper pictures that clearly illustrate five of your words.

HEALTH
Sometimes people give us advice to help us get our anger under control. For example, you may be told to "count to ten" before expressing your anger. Make a personal list of ten things that you could do when you're feeling angry, things that may help you calm down before your anger creates an unpleasant situation.

Example: Run to my room and punch my pillow ten times without saying anything.

ESTEEM ENHANCER

Make a list of "Maddening Moments." Rank them in order from the one that would make you most angry to the one that would make you least angry. Compare your ordered list with a friend's list. OR, use the "Maddening Moments" page.

Maddening Moments

Read over the following list of Maddening Moments. Rank them in order from the one that would make you most angry to the one that would make you least angry. Compare your ordered list with a friend's list. Discuss your differences.

_____ The phone rings many times, but every time you answer it, the person hangs up.

_____ Your younger brother spills green paint on your brand-new white bedroom carpet.

_____ Your mom won't let you go to your best friend's birthday party because your room is not clean.

_____ Your best friend won't sit by you at lunch.

_____ Your sister has told the neighbor that you will babysit for her child on Saturday, and you have already made other plans.

_____ You fell down and twisted your ankle and now you can't participate in the final soccer game with the rest of your team.

_____ Your mom gives you a lunch that has a sandwich that you can't stand and no dessert.

_____ Your family has decided to move to another part of the country and you must move at the end of the month.

_____ You have just torn your brand-new shirt, and you know that your parents will be upset with you.

_____ You have a hard time sleeping because your neighbor plays loud music night after night, and now you're having a difficult time staying awake at school.

ARGUMENTS

The Hating Book
by Charlotte Zolotow

Name _____

SUMMARY

A silly misunderstanding almost causes the breakup of a friendship.

VOCABULARY

1. arithmetic
2. whistled

JOURNAL ENTRY

At one time or another all friends have arguments. Tell about an argument that you have had with a friend and how the problem was finally solved.

_____

_____

_____

_____

_____

_____

_____

_____

_____

CURRICULUM INTEGRATION

HEALTH
Even people we care about very much may have habits that annoy us. Describe an annoying habit had by someone you know. Think of at least five things you could do to get the person to change the habit. Describe your five ideas.

WRITING
With a friend, pretend to be the two people in the story who are having the argument. Write letters to each other and try to solve the problem. Read these to the class.

THINKING SKILLS
Make a list of ten things that you might do to let someone know that you would like to be his or her friend.

ESTEEM ENHANCER

What if people had to advertise for their friends? Design a poster that you could use to advertise for a friend. Describe yourself in detail by listing all of your special qualities on the poster. Be sure to draw a picture of yourself and add as many important details as possible.

The Terrible Fight

by Sharon St. Germain

Name _____

SUMMARY

Molly has a silly but very serious argument with her best friend Becky and discovers just how important friendship is in her life.

VOCABULARY

1. balanced
2. boost
3. windowsill

JOURNAL ENTRY

Pretend that you have just had a terrible argument with your best friend. What are some of the things that you would miss most about losing your friend? What would you try to do to make things better between you again?

_____

_____

_____

_____

_____

_____

_____

_____

CURRICULUM INTEGRATION

HEALTH
If you want to have friends, you have to try very hard to be a friend to others. Divide a sheet of paper into halves by folding the paper or drawing a line. On one half of the paper list the qualities that you have that you think make you a good friend. On the other half, list those qualities that you may wish to change in order to become a better friend. Sit down with another friend or an adult and plan a list of things that you could do to improve your ability to make friends.

VOCABULARY DEVELOPMENT
Make as many words as you can by using the letters in the word FRIENDSHIP. Examples: sir, red.

THINKING SKILLS
If you were new in town, where would you go and what would you do in order to try to meet new friends?

ESTEEM ENHANCER

We send cards to the people we care about on special occasions such as birthdays. Design a special "I'm Sorry" card that could be sold by card shops to people who have had arguments and want to make up.

The Quarreling Book
by Charlotte Zolotow

Name _____

SUMMARY

Sometimes the weather or a forgotten kiss or an unintentional unkind word can cause a chain of unnecessary arguments to occur. Luckily, a kind word can also cause another kind word, and a chain of kindness can begin to spread.

VOCABULARY

1. filthy
2. supposed
3. completely
4. unreasonable
5. unpleasant
6. hindquarters
7. pounced
8. grateful
9. glistening

JOURNAL ENTRY

Think of five kind sentences or phrases that you could use today to begin a chain of kindness. Write them here, and tell who you will share each of them with.

_____

_____

_____

_____

_____

_____

_____

CURRICULUM INTEGRATION

SCIENCE/THINKING SKILLS
Weather can very often affect people's moods. Explain how you would feel on a day when the weather is like each of the following:

        a. A bright, sunshiny day

        b. A driving snowstorm

        c. Strong winds, cold temperatures

        d. A 90-degree day

        e. A cool, calm spring day

THINKING SKILLS
In *The Quarreling Book* it was not a person who was responsible for starting the chain of kindnesses; it was the family dog. Brainstorm with a friend to create a list of animals that look like kind animals and a list of animals that don't appear to be at all friendly.

Example:

Friendly-Looking Animals	Unfriendly-Looking Animals
1. Sea Otter	1. Rhinoceros
2.	2.
3.	3.

MATH/SOCIAL STUDIES
The James family had three children in it, and a mom and a dad. Survey your classroom to find out the most common family size. Do you know how to find the "average size"? If you do, find the average.

ESTEEM ENHANCER

Sometimes we forget just how much we enjoy our family and how much they mean to us. We allow ourselves to become involved in petty arguments. Write a poem about family arguments that may help you think about your actions the next time you feel like quarreling.

Example: Sometimes my family's thoughtless
                    And we argue, fuss, and fight,
                    But I'll say this for certain,
                    That it really isn't right.

                    We need to take some time out
                    And reflect on what we do,
                    For then instead of fighting,
                    We'll be saying, "I love you!"

It's Mine

by Leo Lionni

Name _____

SUMMARY

Much to the annoyance of the toad, three neighbor frogs battle daily and noisily over what belongs to each of them personally. As a result of battling a severe storm, they learn of the benefits of sharing.

VOCABULARY

1. rainbow
2. pebbles
3. island
4. quarrelsome
5. quibbled

6. appeared
7. bickering
8. defiantly
9. distant
10. desperately

11. disappear
12. huddled
13. subsided
14. recognized
15. swarms

JOURNAL ENTRY

The frogs in the story behave very rudely toward one another. What would you have said to each of the three about their unacceptable behavior?

_____

_____

_____

_____

_____

_____

_____

CURRICULUM INTEGRATION

RESEARCH
Do some research to find out the differences between frogs and toads. Write down three facts about each one and make a detailed sketch of each.

THINKING SKILLS
Explain the following statement to a friend: *"Mine is a very small word, and ours is a very large word."*

WRITING
Write a mini-manners book for frogs. Include pictures. Use the following chapter headings:

Manners While Eating
Sharing
Care Of Friends
Greeting Strangers
What To Do In Case Of Bad Weather
Proper Frog Fashions

ESTEEM ENHANCER

There are many good rules that are not really written down but are good to know when making friends. One of them is that friends should share. Decide with a group of three or four friends if the following rules of behavior among friends are really good rules or not. Be able to tell why your group made each decision.

1. Friends should never tell secrets that have been shared with them.
2. Friends should help each other at school by giving answers to questions on tests.
3. Friends should always agree with each other.
4. If a friend is rude to you, you should talk to him or her about the behavior.
5. Girls should never call boys on the phone.

Faye And Dolores

by Barbara Samuels

Name _____

SUMMARY

Faye and Dolores are sisters who have a wonderful time together most of the time. Like all sisters, however, they have arguments and misunderstandings now and then.

VOCABULARY

1. favorite
2. decided
3. pretend
4. library
5. librarian
6. ordinary
7. sardine
8. asparagus
9. decoration
10. delicious
11. disgusting
12. crocodile
13. hamper
14. bulgy

JOURNAL ENTRY

Faye and Dolores have an argument when Dolores accidentally breaks Faye's new red crayon. Faye ends up shouting at Dolores and telling her that she is dumb. What would have been a better way for Faye to have expressed her feelings to Dolores?

_____

_____

_____

_____

_____

_____

_____

CURRICULUM INTEGRATION

READING
When she was little, Dolores was frightened that a crocodile might be living in the toilet. Find at least two other books with crocodile characters and read them. (One is *Loveable Lyle*, by Bernard Waber, Houghton Mifflin, New York, NY 1962.) Tell a friend about your favorite crocodile story.

ART
Faye and Dolores were drawing flowers until the red crayon broke. Draw the most beautiful flower garden that you can imagine. You may wish to use reference books to help you do your best sketching. Make sure to color your flowers brightly. Frame with a black construction paper frame.

RESEARCH
Dolores once ate nearly half a tube of toothpaste. Research to find out the ingredients in most toothpastes. Are any of the ingredients harmful to people if eaten in large quantities? Design a toothpaste tube that you think would appeal to the buying public. Write a short ad attempting to sell your new product.

ESTEEM ENHANCER

Being a member of a family means that you will share some good times and some not-so-good times. Of course, it would be to everyone's advantage to help things go as smoothly as possible. It is best to have a plan of action when trying to make positive changes. Provide oral or written answers to the following questions.

1. What are two things you like best about each of your brothers and sisters?

2. What are two things you would like to change about each of your brothers and sisters?

PEER PRESSURE

The Berenstain Bears And The In-Crowd

by Stan and Jan Berenstain

Name _____

SUMMARY

Sister Bear learns that it is more important to be yourself than to try to be someone you aren't so that you can be part of the "in-crowd."

VOCABULARY

1. comfortable
2. routine
3. generally
4. relaxation
5. unexpected
6. interesting
7. investigate
8. confused
9. interrupted
10. embarrassed
11. attempt
12. continued
13. tournament
14. exhibition
15. disaster
16. congratulated

JOURNAL ENTRY

Describe a time when you felt pressure to do something you didn't want to do in order to be part of the crowd. How could you have handled it differently?
What lesson did Queenie learn in the story? What did you learn?

_____

_____

_____

_____

_____

CURRICULUM INTEGRATION

ART/THINKING SKILLS
You are a world-famous fashion designer. Design a new fashion accessory that children from the ages of eight to twelve would really want to have. Draw and describe it.

PHYSICAL EDUCATION/ART
During the summer, the playground was an important place for Sister Bear and her friends. Create the ultimate playground that you would want to see in your neighborhood. Draw it and describe its features.

WRITING
Write a newspaper story entitled "In Crowds Are Out-To-Lunch."

ESTEEM ENHANCER

You have been hired to take the place of Ann Landers, who has recently retired. Write your esteem-building advice to answer the following reader questions:

Dear A,

Lucy has been my best friend for the last three years. We also have two good friends, Alison and Lisa, who spend a lot of time with us. We always have a lot of fun together. Whenever Lucy and I are alone, though, she will say mean things about Lisa and Alison. I really like Lisa and Alison a lot, and it hurts me to have Lucy cut them down. When I try to defend them, Lucy ends up getting mad at me and stomping away. What should I do?

Signed,
Confused and Caring

Dear A,

I am ten years old, and I don't seem to be able to do anything right. My mom and dad are always yelling at me because my grades aren't good enough. My teacher is always yelling at me to pay attention, and I don't really have any friends that I can talk to. I really want to change, but every time I try, I seem to fail. What should I do?

Signed,
Wants to Change

Ira Sleeps Over

by Bernard Waber

Name _____

SUMMARY

Ira has been invited to spend the night at a friend's house for the very first time. He worries about how his friend will feel about his Teddy bear Tah Tah.

VOCABULARY

1. invited
2. probably
3. suppose
4. decided
5. collection
6. dominoes
7. suddenly
8. mustache
9. haunting

JOURNAL ENTRY

Tell about your favorite stuffed animal or animals. Why do you think that almost every kid likes stuffed animals at some time during his or her life?

_____

_____

_____

_____

_____

_____

_____

_____

CURRICULUM INTEGRATION

THINKING SKILLS

Spending the night with a friend can be a great deal of fun. If you didn't have to worry about the cost, how would you plan an ideal sleepover at your house? Begin the sleepover at 6:00 p.m. and end it at 10:00 a.m. the following day. Tell exactly what you would do hour by hour. Let your imagination run wild! Keep in mind that Mom and Dad would need to approve of your plans.

ART

You have just been chosen to be the new president of "Parties For Kids," an organization that plans parties for children from the ages of two to eighteen. Design a business card that you could give to prospective clients that would tell something about you and your company.

WRITING

Put yourself in Tah Tah's place. How would you describe a typical day in your life? Write about your day from the Teddy bear's point of view.

ESTEEM ENHANCER

A friend respects things that are important to you (like Teddy bears) and does not try to pressure you to be someone that you're not. On a piece of paper, draw seven overlapping circles to form a "Circle of Friendship." Complete the Circle of Friendship by filling the circles with qualities that people who do not exert peer pressure on their friends should have.

Example:

You Look Ridiculous, Said The Rhinoceros To The Hippopotamus

by Bernard Waber

Name _____

SUMMARY

Hippopotamus learns a very important lesson about life when she tries to become something that she isn't. She learns to be proud of exactly what she is.

VOCABULARY

1. jungle
2. rhinoceros
3. hippopotamus
4. ridiculous
5. absolutely
6. decided
7. opinion
8. glorious
9. continuing
10. leopard
11. magnificent
12. disappear
13. nightingale
14. creature
15. appearance

JOURNAL ENTRY

Write about the things that you like best about yourself. Tell why each quality is of value to you.

_____

_____

_____

_____

_____

_____

CURRICULUM INTEGRATION

THINKING SKILLS

Each animal in the story, with the exception of the hippopotamus, felt that there was something very beautiful and special about himself or herself. The turtle was especially proud of its shell. The shell provided protection from the weather and a place to hide. Brainstorm with a friend to think of as many uses as possible for a turtle's shell. Make a list of your ideas. Illustrate your favorite idea.

RESEARCH/ART

Draw a picture of the animal that you consider to be the most beautiful animal in the world. Draw this animal in its natural habitat. Do some research; on the back of the drawing write two facts that you learn about the animal.

SOCIAL STUDIES

Do some research to find out which country or countries each of the following is found in naturally (not in captivity).

1. elephant
2. seal
3. otter

4. ibex
5. jaguar
6. quail

7. reindeer
8. tiger
9. bighorn sheep

ESTEEM ENHANCER

The best way to stand up against peer pressure is to feel good about yourself. Feeling good about yourself is the best gift you can give yourself. Create a great gift to give yourself by completing the worksheet "My Gift To Myself."

My Gift To Myself

A Gift for Myself

I am good at...

I am kind when...

I do a good job at...

I help at home by...

I look good when...

This is how I look...

My friends are...

In school I'm great at...

Two Strikes, Four Eyes

by Ned Delaney

Name _____

SUMMARY

Toby feels that wearing glasses would cause his friends to make fun of him and call him Sissy or Four Eyes. He discovers, however, that his ball team doesn't judge him by his glasses.

VOCABULARY

1. spectacular
2. grounders
3. sprained
4. connect
5. infield
6. dreaded
7. physical
8. exercises
9. fortunately
10. dugout
11. squinting
12. resounding
13. astonished
14. appreciation

JOURNAL ENTRY

Describe how you feel about people who wear glasses. Why do you think that kids are sometimes afraid to wear their new glasses in front of their friends at school?

_____

_____

_____

_____

_____

_____

_____

CURRICULUM INTEGRATION

ART/THINKING SKILLS
Pretend that you are in charge of designing glasses for each of the students in your classroom. Draw and color a pair for one of your friends. Tell about any special features that the glasses might have.

ART
Baseball uniforms are specially designed to prevent as many injuries as possible to the ball players. Each baseball uniform and hat has a logo or uniquely-designed team name placed somewhere on the shirt and hat. Choose a team name for a baseball team that would be composed of the members of your class. Then create a design for a logo using that name.

RESEARCH/THINKING SKILLS
Brainstorm a list of all the sporting activities that you can think of. You may use reference books. After the list is complete, rank order the list from favorite to least favorite.

ESTEEM ENHANCER

Peer pressure plays a big part in how we dress, how we style our hair, the toys that we play with, the music we listen to, and even the way that we speak. Our decisions are greatly influenced by our peers. We also influence the decisions that our friends make. Create a picture of the peers that influence you most. Next to it, draw a picture of the friends that you feel you influence. Label each picture.

The Big Orange Splot

by Daniel Pinkwater

Name _____

SUMMARY

Mr. Plumbean shows his individuality by designing a house to suit his taste, not that of his neighbors.

VOCABULARY

1. seagull
2. explosion
3. steamshovels
4. muttering
5. carpenter
6. hawser
7. decided
8. belfry

JOURNAL ENTRY

In what ways does your home seem to suit the needs of your family? How would you improve it if you could change it in any way that you would like?

_____

_____

_____

_____

_____

_____

_____

CURRICULUM INTEGRATION

WRITING/THINKING SKILLS
A problem occurs in the story when a seagull carrying a can of orange paint drops the can over Mr. Plumbean's house, causing a big orange splot to appear on the house. Until that happens, everyone in the neighborhood has had an identical house. The problem allows Mr. Plumbean an opportunity to express himself as an individual. Create a new problem that Daniel Pinkwater could have written into his story instead of the paint-carrying seagull. Write your new version of "The Big Orange Splot."

ART
If the people on your street were not under any pressure from the neighbors to keep their houses looking a certain way, how do you think their houses might look? Draw your ideas.

RESEARCH/WRITING
Do some research to find out about seagulls. Write two paragraphs of information in your own words to tell some things that you didn't know about seagulls. Illustrate your report.

ESTEEM ENHANCER

We all make decisions of various types every day, many times during the day. Our friends sometimes convince us to do things that we might not otherwise do. This is called peer pressure. In order to make sensible decisions, we need to be sure that what we are doing is our own decision or that of a responsible adult. Fill out the chart entitled WHO MAKES THE DECISION?

Who Makes The Decision?

Decide who should be involved in helping you make the decisions listed below—your parents, your friends, or you alone. Compare your list with a friend's list and discuss.

DECISION	DECISION MAKER
1. Whether or not you should go to school.	
2. What to eat.	
3. What to wear.	
4. How to style your hair.	
5. Who your friends should be.	
6. The books you read.	
7. The TV shows you watch.	
8. Who you write letters to.	
9. How many times you chew your food.	
10. The color of your tennis shoes.	
11. The kind of pop you drink.	
12. The toys you play with.	
13. The time you go to bed.	
14. Whose house you play at most often.	
15. Who to sit by at lunchtime.	
16. Who to play with at recess.	
17. Where to go on vacation.	
18. How your signature should be written.	
19. How late to stay up at a sleepover.	
20. What your favorite color should be.	

FEAR

There's An Alligator Under My Bed

by Mercer Mayer

Name _____

SUMMARY

A fun-filled, fear-conquering frolic that shows children how to get rid of an alligator under the bed.

VOCABULARY

1. alligator
2. bait
3. garage
4. vegetables

JOURNAL ENTRY

Write about something that has frightened you at night. Tell how you overcame your fear.

_____

_____

_____

_____

_____

_____

_____

_____

CURRICULUM INTEGRATION

RESEARCH
Do some research to find out what alligators really do like to eat. Prepare a menu for the newly-opened restaurant "Chez Alligator."

SCIENCE
Find out if alligators are considered an endangered species. Then list as many animals as you can that are also members of endangered species.

THINKING SKILLS
Some animals make better pets than others. Rank the following animals in the order that you would choose them for pets. Give one reason each animal would make a good pet and one reason each animal would not make a good pet.

Goat	Lizard	Giraffe
Pig	Gerbil	Piranha
Mallard	Parrot	Otter
Leopard	Seal	Horse

ESTEEM ENHANCER

People handle fear in different ways. If it is dark in your room and you are afraid of something that you cannot see, you may simply choose to turn on the light. What would you do in each of the following situations in order to keep from becoming too afraid?

1. You are afraid of heights and your best friend has convinced you to take a ride on the world's tallest ferris wheel.

2. You are walking home from a friend's house and you get terribly lost. It is beginning to get dark outside.

3. You are spending your first night away from home and you are afraid of total darkness. Your friend doesn't like to sleep with any lights on.

4. You have just gotten to your first tennis lesson and there is no one that you know in the group.

5. It is your first day of school in a brand-new city where your father has recently been transferred by his company. Nobody speaks your language.

Arthur's April Fool

by Marc Brown

Name _____

SUMMARY

Arthur is so frightened by bully Binky Barnes that he has a hard time practicing his magic tricks for the school assembly. With some special April Fool Magic, however, Arthur soon tricks even Binky.

VOCABULARY

1. telescope
2. threatening
3. practicing
4. assembly
5. Godzilla
6. pulverize
7. barged
8. assistant
9. auditorium
10. volunteer
11. pipsqueak
12. disappear

JOURNAL ENTRY

Write about an April Fool's joke that you have played on someone or one that someone has played on you. If you have never been involved with April Fool's jokes, what would be a good, harmless, humorous joke that you could play?

_____

_____

_____

_____

_____

_____

CURRICULUM INTEGRATION

THINKING SKILLS

Compare and contrast the characteristics of Arthur and Binky. How are you like Arthur? Different? How are you like Binky? Different?

WRITING

Pretend that you are on stage getting ready to perform your famous "Pull the Rabbit from the Hat" trick when a small fairy flies by your ear and whispers that you can pull any three things from the hat that you could possibly wish for. There are only two rules. The wishes must be for items smaller than the hat, and you cannot wish for money or more wishes. What three things would you choose to pull from the hat? Explain why you have chosen each item.

ART

Create a new friend for Arthur who could appear in other Arthur books. Draw Arthur's new friend and tell some things about him or her.

ESTEEM ENHANCER

Bullies like Binky don't begin life wanting to become bullies. Oftentimes, they don't feel very good about themselves and end up bullying others. We can help others to feel better about themselves by coming up with positive comments that we can say when we pass each other in class, in the hall, and on the playground. If we put some time and energy into developing a list of Esteem-Enhancing statements, and refer to it from time to time, we can not only make others feel better, but make ourselves feel better as well.

Example:
ESTEEM ENHANCERS

You look nice today.

Have a good day.

Let's help each other.

I'm Coming To Get You

by Tony Roxx

Name _____

SUMMARY

Young Tommy discovers that reading scary stories about monsters just before bedtime is not a very good idea. Tommy also discovers an interesting truth about monsters during the daylight hours.

VOCABULARY

1. galaxy
2. loathsome
3. statues
4. nibbling
5. radar
6. pounced

JOURNAL ENTRY

Why is it not a good idea to read a scary story or look at a scary TV show just before bedtime? Tell about the scariest story or TV show that you have ever heard or seen.

_____

_____

_____

_____

_____

_____

_____

CURRICULUM INTEGRATION

ART
Draw the meanest, scariest monster that you can think of. Add as much detail as possible. Tell about the monster's personality.

MATH
Write five original Monster Math Problems. Put the answers to the problems on a separate sheet. Put each of the problems into story-problem form, and write each one of them on a monster-shaped card. See if a friend can solve your problems.

Example: Two hairy monsters rushed over to the bakery early one morning to buy some breakfast treats. Hortense bought twelve jelly doughnuts and sixteen cream puffs. Hermione bought fifteen bear claws, eight croissants and eleven bismarcks. How many breakfast treats did they buy altogether?

RESEARCH
How often are frightening television shows available for children to watch during the hours of 6:00 a.m. and 10:00 p.m.? Check out the TV program listing for a one-week period of time. How many scary programs do you find? Over two weeks of time, how many scary programs do you find? What is the average number per week?

ESTEEM ENHANCER

Create your own Monsterbag puppet. Make it scary, hairy, and mean. Then create a Gary Good Guy or Gloria Good Girl bag puppet. With a friend, create a short play in which the good puppet no longer is afraid of Monsterbag.

Because Of Lozo Brown

by Larry L. King

Name _____

SUMMARY

A young boy is afraid of his new neighbor, who he fears will be mean and frightful. He's in for a pleasant surprise when he finally meets Lozo Brown.

VOCABULARY

1. dare
2. pirate
3. gobbles
4. ruffled
5. vanish
6. tropical fish

JOURNAL ENTRY

Who is your favorite neighbor? Why do you like him or her? What kind of neighbor are you?

_____

_____

_____

_____

_____

_____

_____

_____

CURRICULUM INTEGRATION

SOCIAL STUDIES
Lozo is an unusual name for a boy. Take a survey of your classmates. If they could have chosen their own names, what names would they have chosen? How many students would have chosen the names they currently have? What is the most popular boy's name and girl's name chosen by your classmates?

RESEARCH
Do some research to find the following information in your local telephone book:

   a. What last name is found most often in your phone book?
   b. What is the most unusual name that you found?
   c. What is a last name that has four or more syllables?
   d. Are there last names that begin with every letter of the alphabet? If not, which letters are missing?

WRITING
Create a new ending for the story, using a girl as the new neighbor instead of Lozo Brown. You may or may not choose to do it with rhyming verse.

ESTEEM ENHANCER

Sometimes we are afraid of people simply because we do not know them. Choose someone from the class that you do not know very well and ask each other the following questions. (One will ask the even-numbered questions, one the odd-numbered.)

   1. What is your favorite book? Tell me about it.
   2. How would you spend $1000?
   3. Tell me a joke.
   4. Tell me about your favorite class.
   5. What is your most difficult class? Why?
   6. When is your birthday? What gift do you most want?
   7. Tell me about a hobby of yours.
   8. What is your favorite TV show? Tell me why.
   9. Tell me about your pets.
   10. Tell me about your favorite vacation.
   11. What is your favorite holiday? Why?
   12. Tell me about your family.
   13. What entertainer would you like to meet?
   14. What is your middle name?

Who's Afraid Of The Dark?

by Crosby Bonsall

Name _____

SUMMARY

A young boy voices his own fear of the dark with ideas that concern his pet dog, Stella.

VOCABULARY

1. protect
2. shivers

JOURNAL ENTRY

Why do you think people are afraid of the dark? What are some things that you can do to get over a fear of the dark?

_____

_____

_____

_____

_____

_____

_____

_____

CURRICULUM INTEGRATION

RESEARCH
Do some research to find information on animals that would make good guards for people who may be frightened when it gets dark. Tell as much as you can about one of the animals by writing a short report in your own words. Illustrate.

READING
Read another story that features a dog as one of the main characters. How is Stella like the dog in your new story? How are the dogs different?

WRITING
Use old magazines or newspapers to find a picture of a person who has a look of fear on his or her face. Cut it out. Then write a story about why the person is frightened and how he or she got over being afraid.

ESTEEM ENHANCER

Bring in an old but usable pillow case that you are permitted to draw on. You will be using fabric crayons for this activity. It is nice to have a friend to rely on when we are feeling afraid of the dark, so today we are going to create "Fearless Friend." Fearless Friend will be a cheerful character who is capable of chasing away fears in the dark. Just draw Fearless Friend onto your pillowcase and place the case onto your pillow. When you are feeling frightened, you can turn your pillow over and see Fearless Friend. Sketch your idea on paper before actually drawing it on the pillowcase.

The Good-Bye Book

by Judith Viorst

Name _____

SUMMARY

It is sometimes frightening for children left with a babysitter to accept the fact that they must stay home when their parents are out for the evening. This light-hearted look at an age-old dilemma may make that separation easier to take

VOCABULARY

1. French restaurant
2. vegetables
3. temperature

JOURNAL ENTRY

It is important for parents to have time alone together. If you were a parent, what would you do to prepare your children for staying with a babysitter so that they would not be frightened by your leaving?

_____

_____

_____

_____

_____

_____

_____

CURRICULUM INTEGRATION

THINKING SKILLS
Brainstorm with a partner to come up with a list of excuses that you could use when trying to convince your parents not to go out for the evening without you. Do not use excuses that are found in the book. After you have listed at least ten good excuses, rank them from best idea to least favorite idea.

LANGUAGE ARTS
Find the hidden feelings in the sentences below. Example: He loves to gol(f ear)ly in the day.

    a. "Why is the spaghetti all over the wall?" Mom asked.
    b. James looked at his bike's wheel and asked, "Why did it rust?"
    c. "I'm on a special diet and need a sugar-low or rye bread for my sandwich," she told the waitress.

Create two sentences of your own that contain hidden feelings.

WRITING
Babysitters become very important when Mom and Dad go out for the evening. Create a list of Ten Babysitting Rules that all babysitters should be required to follow.

ESTEEM ENHANCER

Create a Fearful Face silhouette of yourself. With a partner, trace each others' silhouettes onto dark paper. Inside your silhouette attach squares of paper that name things that cause fear for you. Your partner should do the same. Then ask your partner to think of ideas that would help you to be less afraid of each item, and tape the fear-buster papers on top of each fear. You should do the same for your partner.

FAMILY

I Hate My Brother Harry

by Crescent Dragonwagon

Name _____

SUMMARY

Harry and his younger sister have problems getting along. Harry uses his big-brother-bully techniques to convince her that he has spit in the pudding and put frog frosting on the brownies. Then he won't let her even touch his trains. A truly delightful story of normal rivalry among siblings.

VOCABULARY

1. electric
2. ruining
3. embarrassed
4. pretends
5. dislike
6. index finger
7. smother
8. stuffed

JOURNAL ENTRY

It is natural for brothers and sisters to argue at times. Write about a disagreement that you have had with a brother or sister. How could you have handled things differently so that you would not have ended up disagreeing?

_____

_____

_____

_____

_____

_____

_____

CURRICULUM INTEGRATION

THINKING SKILLS
Harry's little sister gives him a "secret test" to find out if he wants to be her friend. Design your own secret test. Write about it. You may wish to try it out on a friend or a brother or sister.

HEALTH
It is apparent that Harry really does care about his little sister, through some of the things that he does for and with her. For example, he walked to the library to get library books for her when she had chicken pox. What are some of the ways that you let people in your family know that you care about them? List them.

SCIENCE
Sometimes Harry adds lots of bubble bath to his little sister's bath water and pretends to be a seal. Bubble-making is fun for kids of all ages. Using plastic straws, create your own special bubble-blowing wand. Design it in any shape you prefer. Using a commercial bubble-blowing liquid, give your new wand a try. What kind of bubbles do you think your wand will produce? How correct is your prediction?

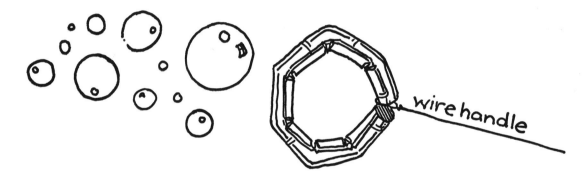

ESTEEM ENHANCER

It is important to our own growth to be valued by others. Likewise, it is important for us to show others that we value and care for them. Create a slogan that will help remind you of the importance of your brothers, sisters, or other family members in your life.

Example:

Now One Foot, Now The Other

by Tomie dePaola

Name _____

SUMMARY

Young Bobby's best friend is his grandfather Bob. Bob taught Bobby to walk. After Bob's stroke, Bobby teaches Bob to walk.

VOCABULARY

1. amusement park
2. phonograph
3. stroke
4. recognize
5. upset

JOURNAL ENTRY

Bobby was greatly influenced by the love of his grandfather Bob. Think about a family member or members who have had a great deal of influence on your life. Tell about them and why they are special to you.

_____

_____

_____

_____

_____

_____

_____

CURRICULUM INTEGRATION

MATH/SOCIAL STUDIES
Take a survey of your classmates to find out how old they were when they learned to walk. Present your information in chart or graph form.

RESEARCH
Grandparents are cared for differently in different countries. Do some research to find out how the people of Japan feel about their grandparents.

SOCIAL STUDIES/ART
Create a generation-to-generation family portrait. Include your brothers or sisters, your parents, your grandparents, and even great-grandparents if possible. Pencil sketch your portrait. Then use watercolor paints for color. After your painting is complete, outline and add detail with black ink or permanent marker. Indicate who the people in your picture are by listing them on the back of your paper.

ESTEEM ENHANCER

Sometimes when people become older, they feel lonely or neglected because they can't be as actively involved in things as they once were. Take time to write a special I-Care-O-Gram to each of your grandparents, letting them know that you are thinking about them. If you don't have grandparents, choose another member of the family to write to.

The Perfect Family

by Nancy Carlson

Name _____

SUMMARY

Louanne Pig discovers that she already has a perfect family after spending the weekend with her friend George and his nine brothers and sisters.

VOCABULARY

1. perfect
2. adopting
3. ignore
4. discovery
5. announced

JOURNAL ENTRY

If you could add more brothers or sisters to your family, how many would you add? How old would they be? Why would you make your choices?

_____

_____

_____

_____

_____

_____

_____

_____

_____

CURRICULUM INTEGRATION

WRITING
Create a story about Louanne Pig by using at least four of the elements listed below. Remember that your story will need characters, a setting or place, a problem, and a solution.

> A family of hippos
>
> A bicycle race
>
> New York City
>
> Extra large tomatoes
>
> Tyro, the circus elephant
>
> A flat tire

RESEARCH
Louanne Pig really liked jelly beans. Do some research to find out what pigs on the farm really do eat. How are pigs and hogs different?

READING
Read three more books written by Nancy Carolson. Choose your favorite character from the books you read. Tell why the character is your favorite. What characteristics does the character have that you admire?

ESTEEM ENHANCER

Plan a Family Esteem-Building Calendar on which you chart ideas to help your family become more perfect together.

Complete the calendar by charting ideas for building family esteem.

Family Esteem Calendar

MONDAY	TUESDAY	WEDNESDAY	THURSDAY	FRIDAY	SATURDAY	SUNDAY

Sheila Rae The Brave

by Kevin Henkes

Name _____

SUMMARY

Sheila Rae is brave and fearless, unlike her scaredy-cat sister Louise. When Sheila finds herself lost, however, the tables quickly turn.

VOCABULARY

1. attacked
2. growled
3. bared
4. pretended
5. occurred
6. families
7. frightening
8. horrible
9. imagined
10. convince
11. fearless
12. dashed

JOURNAL ENTRY

Describe a time when you have felt very brave. Then list the ingredients that you feel go into making up bravery.

_____

_____

_____

_____

_____

_____

_____

CURRICULUM INTEGRATION

SOCIAL STUDIES
Superstitions are fictitious rules that are based on suspicions rather than facts and have been handed down from generation to generation. One superstition says that if you step on a crack, you'll break your mother's back. Of course, we know this has no basis in fact. Write about another superstition that you know. Then tell how our lives would change if the superstition was indeed a fact rather than just fiction. Draw a picture of your realistic superstition.

RESEARCH
The cartoon-like mice that help bring this story to life are not like real mice in many ways. Do research to find answers to the following questions about mice:

1. How big do adult mice get?
2. What do mice eat?
3. How long do mice live?
4. Where do mice usually live?
5. Why do people dislike having mice in their homes?

HEALTH
Sheila Rae bravely faced many things. Sometimes, however, there are things that we should be afraid of for our own safety. List ten things that you feel it is wise to be afraid or cautious of.

Example: Strangers who try to convince you to go someplace with them.

ESTEEM ENHANCER

Sometimes brothers and sisters "bug" each other with the things they do or say. Oftentimes neither person wishes to make the other one angry or upset. List the things you do to "bug" a brother or sister on the Love Bug, then list ideas for "debugging."

Love Bug

List the things that you do to "bug" a brother or sister on the left side of the Love Bug.

List the changes that you could make to "de-bug" your relationship on the right.

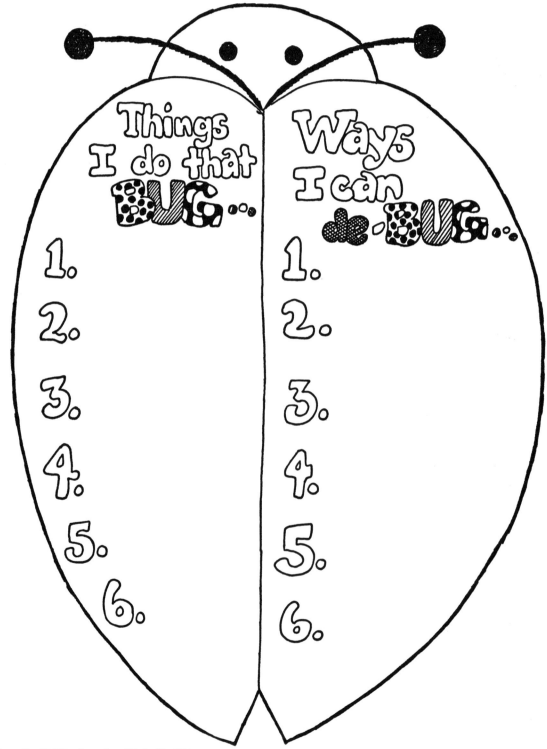

Annie And The Old One

by Miska Miles

Name _____

SUMMARY

In Annie's Navajo world, there is time for all things to return to the earth. When the Old One tells her family that she, too, will return to the earth when the woven rug is completed, Annie tries to prevent its completion.

VOCABULARY

1. Navajo
2. mesa
3. hogan
4. tassels

5. skittered
6. warp
7. weft
8. harmony

9. dawdled
10. timidly
11. trudged
12. gnarled

JOURNAL ENTRY

How is Annie's life in the Navajo world different from your life? What parts of Navajo life would you like to include in your life?

_____

_____

_____

_____

_____

_____

_____

CURRICULUM INTEGRATION

SOCIAL STUDIES
Construct a map of the United States showing where the Navajo people live today.

WRITING
Conduct an interview with a person who is over fifty years old. Prepare at least 15 interview questions in advance to help gather information about the person's childhood, teenage years, and adulthood. Find out about such things as favorite teachers, hobbies, heroes, and advice for living. Then write a story about your older friend's life to share with the class.

READING
Find another book in the library that deals with an Indian family. Read the story, then compare it to *Annie And The Old One*. How are the main characters alike? How are they different?

ESTEEM ENHANCER

The American Indian has played a major role in the history of the United States. Within a cooperative group, research the past history of the Iroquois, Sioux, Pueblo, or Navajo. Find out about their traditions, religions, homes, work, and family life. With your group, put together one of the following:

1. A dialogue that details *positive* contributions your chosen Indian group has made to life in the United States
2. Write a section of information that could be included in an American Indian history book. The section should be approximately two pages long and should detail positive ways the American Indian has affected our life in the Unite States.

Even If I Did Something Awful

by Barbara Shook Hazen

Name _____

SUMMARY

When a young girl plays ball in the living room and breaks her mother's special birthday vase, she needs to be reassured and comforted that her mother will always love her.

VOCABULARY

1. crayoned
2. Empire State Building
3. accident
4. disobeying
5. dessert

JOURNAL ENTRY

Write about a time when you disobeyed a rule and something went wrong because of it. How do you feel you should have been disciplined?

_____

_____

_____

_____

_____

_____

_____

_____

CURRICULUM INTEGRATION

VOCABULARY DEVELOPMENT
The author uses words such as "sloshed" and "swishing" to describe the movement of the bathwater. List at least ten words that describe ways in which water can move. Draw pictures of each one.

THINKING SKILLS
The author gives examples of some phrases said in anger, such as "I told you a thousand times." Create an Angry/Less Angry phrase book that contains six or more phrases that people use when they're angry with one another and six less-angry phrase choices that could be used instead.

Example:

ANGRY	LESS ANGRY
Don't you ever listen?	Remember that it's important to listen to the rules. Fewer accidents happen when we listen.

MATH
Create a math story problem with "a bundle" and "a bunch" in it. Provide an opportunity for the problem-solver to use at least two math processes in the problem. Draw a picture to go with the problem.

ESTEEM ENHANCER

Even when we are careful, accidents may happen or things may not go the way we plan them. If you were a parent, what kind of punishment would you give your child for each of the following situations and why?

1. Your daughter has been told many times not to eat or to drink her pop in her bedroom with its new white carpet. One day, however, she drinks root beer in her room with her girlfriends and accidentally spills her whole glass on the rug. What do you do?

2. Your daughter has forgotten to do her homework for the third time, and the teacher has had to call home to tell you that she is failing her science class. What do you do?

3. Your son has promised you that he will clean the garage with you on Saturday. He and his friends have been working on their bikes in the garage and have created quite a mess. On Saturday morning when you get up, you notice that your son has sneaked out of the house. He doesn't return home until 9:00 p.m. What do you do?

DIVORCE

The Visitors Who Came To Stay

by Annalina McAfee and Anthony Browne

Name _____

SUMMARY

Katy is content to live with her dad with his quiet weekly routine after the divorce of her parents. When Sean and Mary come to stay, she finds that she resents having to share her dad, her home, and her peace and quiet.

VOCABULARY

1. whirligig
2. giddy
3. bustling
4. occasional
5. appetite
6. particularly
7. impressed
8. berets
9. gradually
10. suggested

JOURNAL ENTRY

Katy enjoyed having a regular routine to her week—TV and a story each evening, and cheese sandwiches and an apple for lunch on Monday and Friday. What are some of your favorite routines each week? What would you like to do on a regular basis during the week that you do not do now?

_____

_____

_____

_____

_____

_____

CURRICULUM INTEGRATION

SOCIAL STUDIES

Using pictures from magazines or newspapers, or pictures that you have hand-drawn, create an album that clearly shows an average week in your life. Write a caption for each picture.

WRITING

Make a Wanted Poster for Sean. Include picture, description, and information on the crime, when and where last seen, and reward.

READING

Katy's favorite book is "What Katy Did Next." See if you can find a book with your name in the title. Read it to see if you enjoy it.

ESTEEM ENHANCER

Survey your class to find out which of these three statements they believe:

1. Parents should never be allowed to get a divorce.
2. Parents should be allowed to get a divorce whenever they want to.
3. Parents should try to work things out whenever possible, but should be allowed to get a divorce only as a last resort, when serious problems cannot be solved.

Create a graph that shows the number of classmates who believe each statement.

One More Time

by Louis Baum

Name _____

SUMMARY

Simon and his dad have a comfortable day together before Simon returns home to his mother, with whom he lives.

VOCABULARY

1. station
2. countryside
3. distant
4. twinkle

JOURNAL ENTRY

Simon and his dad enjoyed a wonderful day together. Describe how you would spend a day with your dad if you could plan the whole day and do whatever you wanted to do. (If it wouldn't be possible to plan a day with your dad, plan a day with another favorite adult.)

_____

_____

_____

_____

_____

_____

_____

_____

CURRICULUM INTEGRATION

SCIENCE
In the story, Simon and his father ride the train. In the years to come, we will be forced to develop newer, more efficient types of travel. We will need to take into account energy efficiency, pollution, and cost of operation. Design a method of future travel that will be an improvement over the types of travel that we currently have. Draw your vehicle and write a brief description of its features.

POETRY
Write an 8 to 10 line poem that explains how you feel about divorce.

THINKING SKILLS
During a long trip in a car, plane, or train, it is fun to play games to help pass the time. Create a new game that you could play while traveling.

ESTEEM ENHANCER

When families go through divorce, children oftentimes feel depressed, guilty, or of little value. One way to help each of us feel valuable is to take note of some of our special qualities, as well as to deal with fears or insecurities that we may have. Design a chart or poster that includes lists and/or pictures of the following:

Things I like to do
Important people in my life
Things I like
Things that make me happy
Things I worry about
Things I want to improve

Discuss your chart with a friend.

At Daddy's On Saturdays

by Linda Walvoord Girard

Name _____

SUMMARY

Through Katie's eyes, the reader experiences the pain and confusion of divorce and the agony of one parent moving out.

VOCABULARY

1. quarreled
2. practiced
3. jumble
4. confused
5. disappear

JOURNAL ENTRY

Katie's mother and father talked with her honestly about their divorce and the fact that it wasn't her fault in any way. What are some other things that her mother and father could have done or said to make her feel more comfortable with the family changes?

_____

_____

_____

_____

_____

_____

_____

CURRICULUM INTEGRATION

PHYSICAL EDUCATION
Katie's mom helped her learn her new exercise routine. Design a 15-minute exercise workout that would be good for strengthening the heart muscle. Describe each exercise to the class and show an example by doing each exercise briefly.

ART
Design a floor plan for the placement of living room furniture. Use the Student Worksheet.

WRITING
If Katie kept a diary, what do you think she would have written in it on the day that her daddy left? What would her diary say at the end of the story?

ESTEEM ENHANCER

Write a positive paragraph about your family. Do not put the real names of your family members into your story. See if your family can recognize themselves in the story when you bring it home and share it with them. Describe positive ways that you contribute to the family as well.

Floor Plan

Draw the pieces of living room furniture in the place where you would put them, or cut them out to arrange on the floor plan.
Try to keep the size of each piece in mind as you do your arranging.

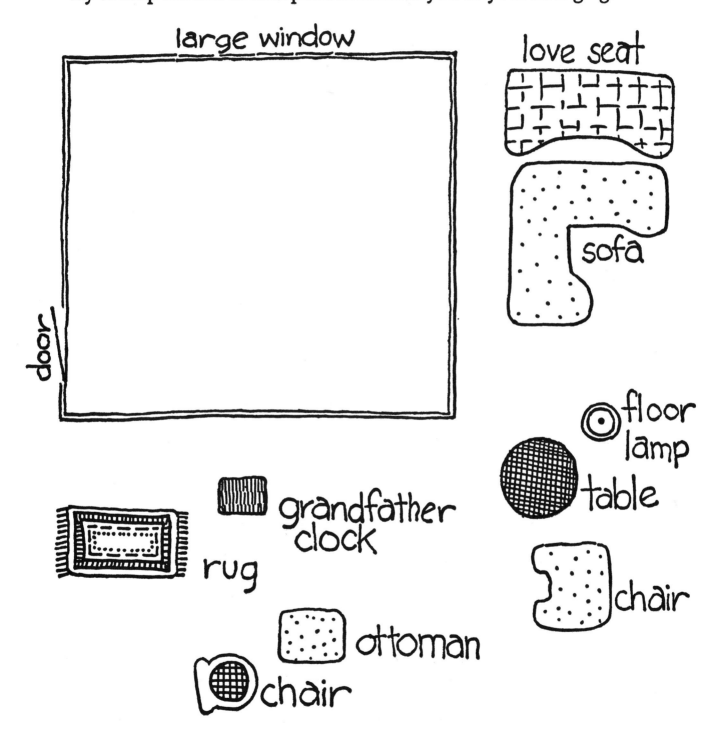

I Wish I Had My Father

by Norma Simon

Name _____

SUMMARY

It is very difficult for a young boy to face Father's Day each year. His father left the family years ago and doesn't write to him or visit him.

VOCABULARY

1. California
2. nickname
3. argue
4. fancy

JOURNAL ENTRY

What kind of assignment would be best for a teacher to give for Mother's Day or Father's Day so that children who live in single-parent families would not feel bad?

_____

_____

_____

_____

_____

_____

_____

_____

CURRICULUM INTEGRATION

ART
The boy in the story drew some special pictures for his grandpa, his friend Jon, and Mr. MacKnight. Draw a special picture for someone important in your life. Color it brightly.

COOPERATIVE WRITING
In groups of four, develop a paragraph from the following topic sentence:

> **It is important for all members of a family to communicate their feelings to one another.**

The topic sentence is given to the first member of the group, who adds a detail sentence after the topic sentence. The paper is then passed to the second member of the group, who adds a second detail. All members contribute one detail sentence. The group finishes by adding a concluding statement that has been formulated by the group. Paragraphs are then shared with the class.

LANGUAGE ARTS
Write a sentence telling how you feel about each of the following topics:

Smiles	Christmas
Friends	Puppies
Broccoli	Computers
Birthdays	Swimming

ESTEEM ENHANCER

The young boy in the story felt sad that his father had been out of his life for so long that he wouldn't even know if his son had a nickname or not. Create a positive nickname for each member of your class.

Example:

| Joan | = <u>Sunshine</u> |

Daddy's New Baby

by Judith Vigna

Name _____

SUMMARY

It is difficult when parents divorce. When a new half-sister comes along, many other adjustments have to be made.

VOCABULARY

1. prepare
2. drowned
3. slope
4. decided

JOURNAL ENTRY

Many more people get divorces today than did fifty years ago. Why do you think there are so many more divorces now? What do you think can be done about the current trend?

_____

_____

_____

_____

_____

_____

_____

_____

CURRICULUM INTEGRATION

SOCIAL STUDIES
What is meant by "half-sister" or "half-brother"? How do you think they got these names? Tell about a half-brother or half-sister that you know. How different are they from just brothers or sisters?

SOCIAL STUDIES
In cooperative groups of three or four, discuss the following: Parents who cannot get along with each other may obtain a divorce; should children ever be allowed to obtain divorces from their parents? Why or why not? After your discussion, present your ideas to another group or to the class.

ART
Kids love having their own rooms. Design the room of your dreams. Draw as many details as you can think of that will make your room as comfortable as possible.

ESTEEM ENHANCER

The young lady in the story loves puppets and puppet shows. Use the finger puppet patterns provided to create a puppet of each of your family members. Using your finger puppets, create a short play about your family's favorite activities for enjoyment and relaxation.

Finger Puppet Patterns

Use the finger puppet patterns to create a puppet of each of your family members. Using your finger puppets, create a short play about your family's favorite activities for enjoyment and relaxation.

LOVE

Love You Forever
by Robert Munsch

Name _____

SUMMARY

The unconditional love of a mother for her son is shown beautifully as they grow together from childhood to old age.

VOCABULARY

teenager

JOURNAL ENTRY

As the young boy in the story grew up, he created a few problems for his mother. These problems may have made her upset with him, but they didn't change her love for him. Tell about some things that you have done that may have driven someone in your family a little crazy.

_____

_____

_____

_____

_____

_____

_____

_____

CURRICULUM INTEGRATION

POETRY/ART
The poem in the book creates a special feeling of love from the mother to her son. Write your own special poem to someone in your family telling about your love for him or her. Then ask someone to trace your profile onto a black sheet of paper as you sit between a light source and the paper. Cut out this black profile and mount it on a white piece of paper. Then mount the poem below your "shadow picture." Give this to the special someone for whom you wrote it.

THINKING SKILLS
You can love someone and not like him or her very much, and you can like someone and not love him or her. Write about the differences between love and like.

WRITING
If the son hadn't had a new baby daughter at home, how could the story have ended? Write a new ending for it.

ESTEEM ENHANCER

You have been chosen to be a guest star on a local talk show, discussing the topic: "Why I'll love my parents always." Draw a picture of yourself on the talk show stage. Then tell or write what you would say to the show's host when she asks you why you will always love your parents.

The Two Of Them

by Aliki

Name _____

SUMMARY

A heartwarming story of the special bond between a grandfather and his granddaughter.

VOCABULARY

1. lullabies
2. bamboo
3. Papouli

JOURNAL ENTRY

Grandfathers and grandmothers help to make up many of our childhood memories. Write about a favorite memory that you have of one or more of your grandparents. You may wish to create a picture to go with your memory.

_____

_____

_____

_____

_____

_____

_____

_____

CURRICULUM INTEGRATION

THINKING SKILLS

You have been chosen to help put together a new, improved, modern-day dictionary to be used in schools across the country. Write out the dictionary entry for the word **love**. When you are done, compare it to the **love** entry in a dictionary found in your classroom.

MATH

Create five math story problems that involve your grandparents or other family members. Put the solutions to the problems on a separate sheet of paper. When you are finished, ask a friend to try to solve the problems.

THINKING SKILLS

Find the hidden family members in the sentences that follow.

Example: His only friend left in a huff when he refused to apologize for being greedy.____son____

1. The crisis terminated their friendship. _____

2. As the oil spills, hot oily broth erodes the landscape of the beach._____

3. "Just put your box of ammo there," said the cowboy.

    _____

4. He could not find his friend's house because he only knew the old address. _____

5. "You are a fun, clever guy," Jill said with delight.

    _____

After you have found answers to the hidden message sentences, create one of your own.

ESTEEM ENHANCER

We can show our grandparents that we care about them and that they are important to us in many ways that don't cost money. List five ways you could let your grandparents know how special they are to you.

Learning About Love

by Jordan Jenkins

Name _____

SUMMARY

Alan Simpson learns a lot about the meaning of the word love when he learns that his mother is ill and needs an operation.

VOCABULARY

1. important
2. x-rays
3. operation

JOURNAL ENTRY

If every person on earth truly felt love for every other person, how would the world change? How would your life be changed?

_____

_____

_____

_____

_____

_____

_____

_____

CURRICULUM INTEGRATION

WRITING/THINKING
Let's pretend that we have a "feelings cookbook" that we can go to in order to cook up different feelings. Turn to the recipe for Love. What will you find on this recipe card? Show what the recipe card for Love looks like in your cookbook.

ART
Create a magazine collage of pictures that show love as you think love might look.

VOCABULARY DEVELOPMENT
List as many words as you can think of that rhyme with "love." After you have completed your list, create a "lovely" poem using at least four of your words.

ESTEEM ENHANCER

Just like Alan Simpson in the story, we sometimes don't take the time to think about how important love is in our lives. To remind our parents of how much we do care for them, we will create a "You Are Special" box for them. Decorate a small box with wrapping paper and ribbon. Inside the box place small cards of brightly-colored paper on which you have written messages that will make Mom and Dad feel special. Then take your "You Are Special" box home and tell Mom and Dad to reach in and pull out a message whenever they need a day-brightener.

The Gnome From Nome

by Stephen Cosgrove

Name _____

SUMMARY

A very cold gnome and otter discover that true warmth is warmth that begins in the heart when we find love and friendship.

VOCABULARY

1. gnome
2. knapsack
3. unanimously
4. skittered
5. appreciation
6. smolder
7. dejected
8. otter
9. tilted
10. exchange
11. rummaged
12. prospector
13. ignored
14. yonder
15. fretted
16. fumed
17. dismay
18. token
19. bonfire
20. Nome

JOURNAL ENTRY

The gnome and the otter found love and "warmth on the inside" because of their friendship. Explain how the people you love make you feel warm on the inside. How do you make other people feel warm on the inside?

_____

_____

_____

_____

_____

_____

CURRICULUM INTEGRATION

POETRY
The story ends with a poem about love and friendship. Create your own poem about love and friendship.

WRITING
Do a three-minute quick-write. List all of the people you love. Then, next to each person, write your favorite memory of him or her. When you have time, you can develop a story about one of the people on your list.

RESEARCH
Do some research to find information about Nome, Alaska. What is the climate like there? How is it different from your climate?

ESTEEM ENHANCER

It is sometimes difficult to tell exactly why we love the people we do. We do know, however, that certain behaviors are more easily accepted than others, and we are more often drawn to those behaviors. Make a list of ten behaviors that you really appreciate in others. When your list is complete, get into a group with three other people and compare lists. Decide which of the behaviors you feel you try to exhibit. Are there positive behaviors that you see as personal strengths that are not on the lists? If so, what are they?

I'll Always Love You

by Hans Wilhelm

Name _____

SUMMARY

When his dog dies peacefully in its sleep, a
young boy is comforted by the knowledge that
he had made sure to say, "I'll always love you," every day.

VOCABULARY

1. mischief
2. scolded
3. difficult
4. vet
5. discovered

JOURNAL ENTRY

Write about a favorite memory that you have of a pet. If you have never had a pet,
tell what type of pet you would like to have some day and why you made your
choice.

_____

_____

_____

_____

_____

_____

_____

_____

CURRICULUM INTEGRATION

RESEARCH
Owning a pet is a big responsibility. When we love our pets, we are responsible for caring for them properly. Do some research to find out all that you would need to do to care for the pet of your choice. Make a chart or report of your research findings, including the following information: type of food pet eats, how often to feed it, type of home required, care of home, grooming needs, exercise and training, veterinary needs, and special concerns.

MATH
Survey the class to find out each classmate's favorite type of pet from the following list: gerbil, dog, cat, hamster, fish, lizard, and bird. Create a graph of your results.

THINKING SKILLS
Brainstorm with a friend to create a list of ways that people and pets are alike. Then, list ways that people and pets are different.

ESTEEM ENHANCER

There are several great comic strips about pets available to us each week (such as Garfield). These comic strips give pets almost human-like characteristics. Design your own lovable comic strip pet. What would be the name of your character? Create a short story about your character in comic strip form. You may wish to use a favorite pet memory to help you with an idea.

WORRY

Harriet's Recital

by Nancy Carlson

Name _____

SUMMARY

Harriet worries continually about being in Miss Betty's dance recital—until she discovers that she can do it after all.

VOCABULARY

1. ballet
2. recitals
3. whispered

4. offstage
5. frightened

JOURNAL ENTRY

People sometimes worry when they have to perform in front of a group or speak before an audience of listeners. Tell about a time when you may have worried about being in front of a group. Why do you think people worry about performing for others?

_____

_____

_____

_____

_____

_____

_____

_____

CURRICULUM INTEGRATION

ART, WRITING
List five worries that you have or have had. Draw a picture of how each one would look if it came to life. What would you say to each of them when you met it for the first time?

PHYSICAL EDUCATION
Create a new dance to go with a favorite song of yours. Share your new dance with a small group or with the class if time permits.

LANGUAGE ARTS
Write four adjectives that could be used to describe a recital of one kind or another.

ESTEEM ENHANCER

Worry causes stress. One way to help eliminate stress is to spend time talking to friends and family members, laughing and sharing ideas and stories. Create a Buddy Book to keep phone numbers and pictures of people you can rely on to talk with (especially when you are feeling worried).

Thornton The Worrier

by Marjorie Weinman Sharmat

Name _____

SUMMARY

Thornton Rabbit passes the time by worrying about everything from toothaches he might get to his house falling down. An older man whose house actually does fall down teaches him much about worrying.

VOCABULARY

1. hippopotamus
2. assorted
3. disasters
4. mountain
5. leaning
6. mending
7. mosquito

JOURNAL ENTRY

It is said that about one third of our time is spent worrying about things that can never be changed, such as past decisions. Less than one-tenth of our time is spent on worry over real concerns ("Will my brother help me study for my science test?"). Write about a worry that you have had that concerns something you could never change no matter how much you worry. Why do you have this worry? How can you stop needless worry?

_____

_____

_____

_____

_____

_____

CURRICULUM INTEGRATION

THINKING SKILLS

Turn worry into happiness by listing as many things as you can that cause you to become happy, using these letters:

W

O

R

R

Y

WRITING

Write a W story that attempts to explain to someone else that he or she shouldn't spend too much time worrying.

> Example: Wally was a worrywart. He worried about weekend walleye fishing, Wednesday weiner roasts, weather-worn wishing wells, and wobbly waffle irons.

ART

Design your own "Worrywart." Explain how owning a Worrywart would help you feel less worried about things.

ESTEEM ENHANCER

People tend to worry about things that never happen, things that can't be changed, how others feel, and a few real or justifiable concerns. It is normal human nature to worry. However, it is also stressful to worry.

One way to help yourself to worry less is to take a good look at the things you worry about. Try to take an objective look at them, then do some problem-solving to act against your worries.

Begin today by listing anything and everything that you are worried about. File the list away. Check next week and see how many of these concerns you still have. Do this for three or four weeks. At the end of this time, evaluate just how important your worries have been. Can you smile now about some of the things that may have worried you earlier? What have you learned about worrying?

Will You Come Back For Me?

by Ann Tompert

Name _____

SUMMARY

Suki worries about going to a child care center when her mother goes to work. Then her mother makes a beautiful red heart and tenderly explains why she will always come back to get her.

VOCABULARY

1. wandered
2. announced
3. bunched
4. tangled
5. bedclothes
6. twisted
7. panda
8. koala
9. supermarket
10. customer

JOURNAL ENTRY

Describe a time when you were worried that your parents wouldn't come back to pick you up. If you were babysitting for a small child who was worried that his mom wouldn't come back for him, what could you do to reassure him?

_____

_____

_____

_____

_____

_____

_____

CURRICULUM INTEGRATION

ART
Suki's mother made a beautiful red heart to show Suki how much she loved her. Create your own red heart with the name of someone you love on it, and tell the person the story "Will You Come Back For Me?" when you give your present.

ART/WRITING
Lulu Bear was Suki's very dear friend. Suki dreamed that she took Lulu to "Brown Bear's School For Teddies." Draw a picture of Brown Bear's School and describe what it would be like there.

SOCIAL STUDIES
What country do you suppose the name Suki comes from? Why did you make your choice? Find the country you chose on the map. What are two other countries located close to it? What is the name of one river in the country? What ocean is it in? Draw the country and label nearby countries, rivers, and oceans.

ESTEEM ENHANCER

List the top five things that worry you the most. Then get together with a partner and search for two ideas or activities that would cause you to worry less about each item on your list. Next time you feel worried, look at your "Fight Back Against Worry" packet and try to fight back.

Example:

FIGHT BACK AGAINST WORRY

Lucretia The Unbearable

by Marjorie Weinman Sharmat

Name _____

SUMMARY

Lucretia is an unbearable hypochondriac with
many an imagined problem to worry about—
until her friends tell her just how unbearable she really is.

VOCABULARY

1. thermometer
2. handkerchief
3. shriveled
4. memory
5. inquired
6. coughed
7. definitely
8. examine
9. certainly
10. mention
11. fester
12. particular
13. fantastic
14. ambulance
15. bunions
16. practically
17. overflowing
18. indigestion
19. unbearable

JOURNAL ENTRY

Write about your worst illness or injury. What happened to you? How did your
family and friends treat you? How did you feel?

_____

_____

_____

_____

_____

_____

_____

CURRICULUM INTEGRATION

ART
Little children love having self-sticking bandages put on their cuts—especially if they are fun to look at. Design a self-sticking bandage that you think little kids would really love to use.

RESEARCH
Do some research to find out the kinds of accidents and illnesses that are the most common among young children. Which are the most dangerous? Interview a public health person by phone, if possible, to help you gather your information.

HEALTH
People in America have different health worries today than they did one hundred years ago. List some diseases that were terribly dangerous about one hundred years ago that we really don't worry about today. Choose one and find out how it became less of a threat to people.

ESTEEM ENHANCER

When someone is worried about something, it is a good idea to try to take that person's mind off that worry. Using magazines or newspapers, clip funny pictures and statements to create a LAUGH A MINUTE poster. Keep the poster in a special place to look at when you are worried or to share with a friend who is worried.

Maggie Doesn't Want To Move

by Elizabeth Lee O'Donnell

Name _____

SUMMARY

Simon voices his fears about moving by making references to his younger sister Maggie. After meeting his new teacher, however, Simon decides that moving isn't so bad after all.

VOCABULARY

1. allowed
2. bawled out
3. smeared
4. bannisters
5. separate
6. shrug

JOURNAL ENTRY

Have you ever moved to a new house? How did you feel? What are the kinds of worries that might be faced by a child who is moving to a new home? How can you be helpful to someone who has just moved to your neighborhood or school?

_____

_____

_____

_____

_____

_____

_____

CURRICULUM INTEGRATION

WRITING
Take off your right shoe and trace a picture of your foot onto white paper. Then write a story about "The First Day In my New School" from a shoe's point of view.

WRITING
Your best friend has just found out that her family is moving to a new home 500 miles away. She seems very sad. Write a letter to cheer her up and help her to feel better about moving.

THINKING SKILLS
If the moving van could not get to your new house for a couple of weeks and each member of your family could take five things with him or her in the car, what five things would you choose to take and why? Remember that they must all fit into the trunk of the car. Do not include things that you would need to wear.

ESTEEM ENHANCER

The song "Don't Worry, Be Happy" tells us to forget about our worries. Write your own song lyrics to convince others not to worry about anything.

Will It Be Okay?

by Crescent Dragonwagon

Name _____

SUMMARY

A young girl is taught by her wise and loving mother to deal with the worries of everyday life.

VOCABULARY

1. perfectly
2. unafraid
3. attention
4. leggings
5. cabbages
6. nursery
7. bandanna
8. thumbnail
9. sensible
10. crackling

JOURNAL ENTRY

Write about something that causes you to worry. Why do you think that you are worried about it? What can you do to worry less?`

_____

_____

_____

_____

_____

_____

_____

CURRICULUM INTEGRATION

RESEARCH
The author of *Will It Be Okay?* uses the pen name Crescent Dragonwagon. Do some research to find out who Crescent Dragonwagon is and what favorite children's author she is related to.

WRITING
This book is filled with What Ifs to worry about—such as what if there is thunder, what if there is lots of snow, and what if you die? Add a new What If to the story. Then explain how you would tell the little girl not to worry about it.

LANGUAGE ARTS
One of the vocabulary words for this story has the prefix UN which often means NOT when placed before a word: UNAFRAID means NOT AFRAID. List as many words as you can think of that have an UN prefix meaning not. Write sentences for three of your words.

ESTEEM ENHANCER

When we are worried or afraid it helps if we try to remember something special that makes us happy. Make up your own DRIVE OUT WORRY poem that you can think about whenever you're worried about something. Example:

> Worry, oh worry, please disappear;
> Be gone from my life for more than a year.
>
> Worry, oh worry, I didn't choose you—
> What I want to do now is simply to lose you.
>
> So out of my life—scram, scoot, scat!
> Now, I am worry-free, just like that.

Bibliography

Alexander and the Terrible, Horrible, No Good, Very Bad Day, Judith Viorst. New York: Macmillan, 1972 (p. 39).

Anna Banana and Me, Lenore Blegvad. New York: Atheneum Books, 1985 (p. 11).

Annie and the Old One, Miska Miles. Boston: Little Brown and Co., 1971 (p. 113).

Arnie and the New Kid, Nancy Carlson. New York: Viking Penguin, 1990 (p. 19).

Arthur's April Fool, Marc Brown. Boston: Little, Brown and Co., 1983 (p. 91).

At Daddy's On Saturdays, Linda Walvoord Girard. Niles, IL: Albert Whitman and Co., 1987 (p. 123).

Attila the Angry, Marjorie Weinman Sharmat. New York: Holiday House, 1985 (p. 55).

Because Of Lozo Brown, Larry L. King. New York: Viking Kestrel, 1988 (p. 95).

The Berenstain Bears and the In-Crowd, Stan and Jan Berenstain. New York: Random House, 1989 (p. 75).

The Big Orange Splot, Daniel Pinkwater. New York: Hastings House, 1977 (p. 84).

The Black Snowman, Phil Mendez. New York: Scholastic, Inc., 1989 (p. 53).

Crabby Gabby, Stephen Cosgrove. New York: Stern, Price, Sloan, 1985 (p. 27).

Daddy's New Baby, Judith Vigna. Niles, IL: Albert Whitman and Co., 1982 (p. 128).

Different, Not Dumb, Margot Marek. New York: Franklin Watts, 1985 (p. 14).

Even If I Did Something Awful, Barbara Shook Hazen. New York: Atheneum Press, 1981 (p. 115).

Everyone Is Special, Marcia Neese. Mankato, MN: Baker Street Productions, 1984 (p. 21).

Faye and Dolores, Barbara Samuels. New York: Bradbury Press, 1985 (p. 71).

A Fish In His Pocket, Denys Cazet. New York: Orchard Books, 1987 (p. 37).

The Gnome From Nome, Stephen Cosgrove. Los Angeles: Price, Stern, Sloan, 1986 (p. 139).

The Good-Bye Book, Judith Viorst. New York: Atheneum Press, 1988 (p. 99).

Grandmama's Joy, Eloise Greenfield. New York: Philomel Books, 1980 (p. 43).

Gus and Buster Work Things Out, Andrew Bronin. New York: Dell Publishing, 1975 (p. 33).

Harriet's Recital, Nancy Carlson. Minneapolis: Carolrhoda Books, Inc., 1982 (p. 145).

The Hating Book, Charlotte Zolotow. New York: Harper Row, 1969 (p. 63).

I Hate My Brother Harry, Crescent Dragonwagon. New York: Harper and Rose, 1983 (p. 103).

I Was So Mad, Mercer Mayer. Wisconsin: Western Publishing Co., 1983 (p. 58).

I Wish I Had My Father, Norma Simon. Niles, IL: Albert Whitman and Co., 1983 (p. 126).

I'll Always Love You, Hans Wilhelm. New York: Crown Publishers, Inc., 1985 (p. 141).

I'll Fix Anthony, Judith Viorst. New York: Harper and Row, 1969 (p. 51).

I'm Coming To Get You, Tony Ross. New York: Dial Books, 1984 (p. 93).

Ira Sleeps Over, Bernard Waber. Boston: Houghton Mifflin Co., 1972 (p. 77).

It's Mine, Leo Lionni. New York: Alfred A. Knopf, 1985 (p. 69).

Learning About Love, Jordan Jenkins. Chicago: Children's Press, 1979 (p. 137).

Love You Forever, Robert Munsch. Ontario: Firefly Books, 1986 (p. 133).

Lucretia the Unbearable, Marjorie Weinman Sharmat. New York: Holiday House, 1981 (p. 151).

Maggie Doesn't Want to Move, Elizabeth Lee O'Donnell. New York: Four Winds Press, 1987 (p. 153).

Making the Team, Nancy Carlson. New York: Puffin Books, 1985 (p. 31).

Nobody's Perfect, Not Even My Mother, Norma Simon. Niles, IL: Albert Whiteman and Co., 1981 (p. 16).

Now One Foot, Now The Other, Tomie dePaola. New York: G.P. Putnam's Sons, 1981 (p. 105).

One More Time, Louis Baum. New York: William Morrow and Co., 1986 (p. 121).

The Perfect Family, Nancy Carlson. Minneapolis: Carolrhoda Books, Inc., 1985 (p. 107).

The Quarreling Book, Charlotte Zolotow. New York: Harper Row, 1963 (p. 67).

Sheila Rae the Brave, Kevin Henkes. New York: Greenwillow Books, 1987 (p. 110).

Sometimes I Like to Cry, Elizabeth and Henry Stanton. Chicago: Albert Whitman and Co., 1978 (p. 41).

Sometimes It's O.K. To Be Angry, Dr. Mitch Golant. New York: Tom Doherty Associates, Inc., 1987 (p. 49).

The Tenth Good Thing About Barney, Judith Viorst. New York: Atheneum, 1984 (p. 45).

The Terrible Fight, Sharon St. Germain. Boston: Houghton Mifflin Co., 1990 (p. 65).

The Terrible Thing That Happened At Our House, Marge Blaine. New York: Four Winds Press, 1975 (p. 29).

There's An Alligator Under My Bed, Mercer Mayer. New York: Dial Books for Young Readers, 1987 (p. 89).

Thornton the Worrier, Marjorie Weinman Sharmat. New York: Holiday House, 1978 (p. 147).

The Two of Them, Aliki. New York: Greenwillow Books, 1979 (p. 135).

Two Strikes, Four Eyes, Ned Delaney. Boston: Houghton Mifflin Co., 1976 (p. 82).

The Visitors Who Came to Stay, Annaline McAfee and Anthony Browne. New York: Viking, 1985 (p. 119).

A Weekend With Wendell, Kevin Henkes. New York: Viking Penguin, 1986 (p. 25).

Who's Afraid of the Dark? Crosby Bonsall. New York: Harper and Row, 1980 (p. 97).

Will It Be Okay? Crescent Dragonwagon. New York: Harper and Row, 1977 (p. 155).

Will You Come Back For Me? Ann Tompert. Niles, IL: Albert Whitman and Co., 1988 (p. 149).

You Look Ridiculous, Said the Rhinoceros To the Hippopotamus, Bernard Waber. Boston: Houghton Mifflin Co., 1966 (p. 79).